what really counts

for women

Presented To:

_____

Presented By:

_____

Date:

_____

what
really
counts
for women

NELSON BOOKS
A Division of Thomas Nelson Publishers
Since 1798

www.thomasnelson.com

Published in Nashville, Tennessee, by Thomas Nelson, Inc.

Managing Editor: Lila Empson
Editor: Kyle L. Olund
Manuscript: Sally Hupp
Design: Thatcher Design, Nashville, Tennessee

Library of Congress Cataloging-in-Publication Data

What really counts for women.
     p. cm.
  ISBN 0-7852-0927-1 (pbk.)
  1. Christian women—Religious life. I. Thomas Nelson Publishers.
  BV4527.W455 2005
  248.8'43—dc22

2005025270

Printed in the United States of America
05 06 07 08 09 QWK 5 4 3 2 1

Life's major pursuit is not knowing
self ... but knowing God ... Unless
God is the major pursuit of our lives,
all other pursuits are dead-end
streets, including trying to know
ourselves.

CHARLES R. SWINDOLL

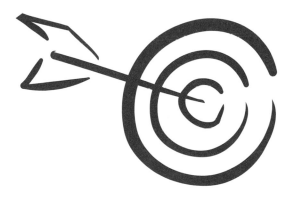

Contents

Introduction

It's a fact: you can't have chocolate-chip waffles without chocolate chips. Even if you have whipped cream, chocolate sauce, and maraschino cherries at the ready, your waffles won't taste right if they're missing that major ingredient. What really counts when making chocolate-chip waffles is a great big heaping helping of chocolate chips.

In the same way, if you want to know what really matters to your life and your faith experience, you need a great big heaping helping of the Bible and God's wisdom. Why? Because God is the One who made you, and He's the one who has some practical, relevant things to say about the things that really count in your life—your health, family, and career; your faith, church, and future; and your understanding of God, Jesus, and the Holy Spirit.

That's where this book fits in. Filled with inspirational stories, thought-provoking quotes, and life-changing Scripture verses, this handbook on life contains the essence of what God has determined really counts in your life experience. You'll find new insights about God's blessings, about the way He wants to work in your life, and about the ways you can grow in your faith.

Yes, it's true: you can't have chocolate chip waffles without chocolate chips. You can't have a fulfilling, joyful, blessed life without God, either. So start mixing up something wonderful in your faith and life. Let God show you *What Really Counts for Women*.

—Sally Hupp

LIFE

An Introduction

> Everything was created through him; nothing—
> not one thing!—came into being without him.
> What came into existence was Life.
>
> JOHN 1:3–4 MSG

Babies are such wonderful creatures. By just drawing their first breaths, these brand-new little persons embody all life's best opportunities. Folks *ooh* and *aah* over these newborns, making observations about family resemblances and speculations about the little one's college and career choices. Just looking at a baby can remind you that once upon a time you, too, were that same size. You used to be that dependent, that impressionable, and that full of possibilities.

Indeed, there are days that you still feel that way, deep down inside, anyway. Yet if you were to stay a baby all your life, think of all the experiences you would miss, all the people you would miss knowing and the relationships you would not form, all the special moments in your life that would not transpire. It is only by growing into the life God has given that one can truly appreciate living moment by moment in His love and care.

The little one nestled in Mom's arms also has no idea about the relationship that can be formed between Creator and created. It is only as the big picture of life unfolds at your feet that you can discover the unique status you possess in God's kingdom. As life happens to you and in you and around you, the fearsomeness of the world melts into the realization of God's greatness and love for you, for all life begins and consists in God. All moments are His. All creation is His. And you and your life are His too.

Life is whatever God wills it; and, such as it is, it's enough!

LEON VAN MONTENAEKEN

Life
More Than a Susan B.

> What are mortals that you should think of us, mere humans that you should care for us?
>
> PSALM 8:4 NLT

If you were to empty your pockets of loose change right now, you might find pennies, nickels, dimes, or a quarter or two. While the size and color of these coins help you determine the worth of each one, the image imprinted on each coin determines its actual monetary value. Though a Susan B. Anthony coin may be the same size and color as a standard-issue Liberty quarter, the image on the Susan B. indicates that this silver dollar is worth four times more than its quarter-sized counterpart.

what really counts

You, too, may share certain characteristics that mark you as a member of your family. You might have your grandmother's nose, your dad's eyes, or your mom's true hair color. But those physical traits, much like the physical characteristics of coins, do not give you an intrinsic worth. Like a coin, you carry an imprint on your life that determines your value, because "when God created people, he made them in the likeness of God. He created them male and female, and he blessed them" (Genesis 5:1–2 NLT). Your life as a woman is precious because you bear the image of God.

Recognizing this truth opens your heart to amazing discoveries about your part in the big picture of life. Your life embodies abundant blessings and responsibilities because of the image you bear. Because you are made in God's likeness, you are more important to Him than anything else in creation. As such, you are to be respected, valued, and esteemed—by yourself and others. Because you bear God's mark on your life, you have a living spirit that can communicate directly with Him. You can be God's friend; no other created being on earth has been granted that privilege. Because you are created in God's image, your life can reflect God's nature—His holiness, compassion, righteousness, and love—in your relationships with others. And, because you are God's image-bearer, He has entrusted you with the lifelong responsibility to care for His creation, to respect and protect all living things—"the world, and those who dwell in it" (Psalm 24:1 NASB).

The loose change in your pocket may have little value, but your life is priceless, of inestimable value because God has stamped His image on you. Look for the daily blessings and responsibilities that come with bearing God's image. And honor God by spending your life wisely as a respected, valued, and esteemed friend of God.

Life
More Than a Susan B.

What Matters Most...

- ◎ Knowing that you bear the image of God in your inner-most heart and soul.

- ◎ Recognizing that you are more valuable to God than anything else in all life and creation.

- ◎ Remembering that you can reflect the aspects of God's nature to others because you bear His image.

- ◎ Understanding that you have a living spirit that can communicate directly with God anytime, anywhere.

- ◎ Spending each moment of your life with a focus on honoring God in all you do.

What **Doesn't** Matter...

- ◎ Which family member you most resemble.

- ◎ How much money you make, spend, or keep in your pockets.

- ◎ Whether or not you feel your life is worthwhile.

- ◎ The old assumption that guys are better than girls. God's image is stamped on all humans—male *and* female.

- ◎ Whether or not people have respected you, valued you, or esteemed you in the past. As God's image-bearer, you can respect yourself and thereby honor Him.

Focus Points...

When God created human beings, he made them in his own likeness. He created them male and female, and on that day he blessed them and named them human beings.
GENESIS 5:1–2 NCV

God created people in his own image; God patterned them after himself; male and female he created them.
GENESIS 1:27 NLT

To kill a person is to kill a living being made in God's image.
GENESIS 9:6 NLT

God is the One who gives life, breath, and everything else to people. He does not need any help from them; he has everything he needs.
ACTS 17:25 NCV

**what
really
counts**

Thou art honored above all creatures in that thou art an image of God ... thou art destined to greatness!
MEISTER ECKHART

You are not only one of God's most carefully and darefully designed creatures, not only one of the strongest, brightest, and best of all creation, you are also the only creature able to know and comprehend God!
ROBERT SCHULLER

Life
In a Moment

O God, remember that my life
is but a breath.

JOB 7:7 NLT

what really counts

Any woman can tell you, moments matter. In a moment, a woman can respond to a call for aid, change her outfit, pull together a fabulous dinner, or settle a world war between coworkers or small children. In a moment, a woman can irretrievably lose a document on a computer, give a compliment that boosts someone's self-esteem, or cry with a friend who needs a broad shoulder. Women innately know that in life, moments matter.

Yet life's moments matter not because of what you can *do* in those little snatches of time. Rather, the moments of your life matter because of God's purpose and plan for your life during your years on this earth. God is at work in all that happens to you, even in the little snatches of time. In fact, in God's economy, your life is one large, God-centered moment in eternity that is meant to bring you closer to Him, to warn you away from harmful, evil things, and to bring about God's best blessings in your life. You may live to be seventy or eighty years old or even older, but all the moments of your life are to be wrapped up in God. All the moments of your life are meant to bring you into a closer relationship with Him.

Consider this: the Bible assures you that He will use every experience in your life for good. It's easy to believe God can work out the moments in your life for good when everything is running smoothly, when, as Browning said, "God's in His heaven—all's right with the world." Yet at times, the moments of your life can be tough ones. God sometimes allows those tough moments to come into your life to correct you, to teach you to trust Him even more, or to bring you back into close fellowship. When God does allow tough moments in your life, choose to trust Him. Choose to believe that He will work everything out for your good, for God promises a wonderful life for all eternity to those who trust Him.

Remember, all the days of your life are God-wrapped moments. In a moment, you can choose to follow Him for a lifetime. In a moment, you can trust Him to bring good out of a bad situation. In a moment, God can change your life. So live your life moment-by-moment for Him.

Life
In a Moment

What Matters Most...

- God's plan and purpose for your life during your years on this earth.

- Knowing that God is at work in all that happens to you.

- Understanding that God wants to bring about good in your life.

- Recognizing that all the moments and experiences of your life are meant to strengthen your relationship with God.

- Being willing to live your life moment-by-moment for God.

What Doesn't Matter...

- How long your life will last.

- How much you can accomplish in the little moments you have every day.

- How tough or easy life is or isn't.

- How many times you've forgotten to trust God to bring good out of bad situations.

- How you've lived your life up until now. Take a moment and let God change your life by choosing to follow Him today.

Focus Points...

What is life? You are a mist that is seen for a moment and then disappears.
JAMES 4:14 GOD'S WORD

We are here for only a moment, visitors and strangers in the land as our ancestors were before us.
1 CHRONICLES 29:15 NLT

"An entire lifetime is just a moment to you; human existence is but a breath ..." And so, Lord, where do I put my hope? My only hope is in you.
PSALM 39:5, 7 NLT

Hour by hour I place my days in your hand.
PSALM 31:15 MSG

Choose to love the LORD your God and to obey him and commit yourself to him, for he is your life.
DEUTERONOMY 30:20 NLT

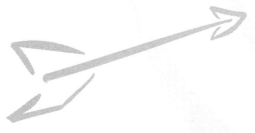

Life is a fragment, a moment between two eternities; influenced by all that has preceded, and to influence all that follows.
WILLIAM ELLERY CHANNING

Our life is scarce the twinkle of a star in God's eternal day.
BAYARD TAYLOR

What Matters Most to Me About
Life

What is life all about? Why are you here? Two simple reasons: to bear God's image and to use life's moments to grow closer to Him. Discover the blessings and responsibilities hidden within these truths as you reflect on the following points.

◎ *Spend a few moments thinking about everything God created. List ways you enjoy what God has made. Then consider, as God's image bearer, ways you could help protect God's creation. What would it take to accomplish these tasks?*

_____

_____

_____

_____

_____

◎ *Make a chart with two columns. In the first column, list God's character traits—love, holiness, and so forth. Because you bear the image of God in your life, use the second column to record ways that each of God's character traits can be physically or spiritually exhibited in your life. How can you implement these ideas?*

_____

_____

_____

_____

_____

⊙ *All your days are God-wrapped moments. Describe a personal experience in which you have clearly sensed God's presence in that exact moment. How did this special time strengthen your relationship with God?*

_____

_____

_____

_____

_____

_____

_____

_____

⊙ *God has given you your life. Yet in the light of eternity, your life is but a brief moment. What do you have to do, change, or adapt in your daily life to make the moments count—right now—in your relationships with God and with others?*

_____

_____

_____

_____

_____

_____

_____

_____

The Spirit of God has made me, and the breath of the Almighty gives me life.
JOB 33:4 NKJV

GOD

An Introduction

> Their Redeemer is strong, the LORD of hosts is His name.
>
> JEREMIAH 50:34 NASB

what really counts

A small, childlike faith sometimes centers on a simple God: He's big; He's in charge; and He seems very busy. While these things may be true, there's a lot more to God. Hidden within the pages of Scripture are metaphors, conversations, and descriptions that can give you a broader understanding of God.

Consider this: as the sovereign Creator of everything, God is powerful. But the scriptural allusions to the big, mighty, powerful God who waves His hand and rules the nations also point to that same big, mighty, powerful God who opens His hand and pours blessings upon His children.

Yet that's only part of it. Hidden within the Bible are also reassurances of God's care for you. You may be waiting longer than you expected for an answer to prayer or a solution to a problem or a situation, but that doesn't mean you are waiting in vain. God has a timetable. Waiting for Him to come to your aid may be necessary. As you wait and glimpse the varied aspects of God's being and character, you learn that God can be trusted to be what His name says He is. You find out that although you may not be able to see God physically until you reach heaven, His face can shine on you right now and bring you peace.

Yes, God is big, and He is in charge. But He cares about you. You are very important to Him. So take some time to get to know God.

Naught but God can satisfy the soul.

PHILIP JAMES BAILEY

God
What's in a Name?

As for our Redeemer, the LORD of hosts is His name, the Holy One of Israel.

ISAIAH 47:4 NKJV

what really counts

What is your name? This may seem like a simple question, but your name may take many forms depending on the situation. You may be "Mommy" to a toddler, "Sweetie" to a spouse, "Kiddo" to a parent, or "Ruth Ann Michaels" to the IRS. Your names—whether nicknames or given names—tell others a lot about you.

Likewise, God has many different names. With God, each name reflects a different facet of His being and character. The titles Lord God Almighty and God Most High signify His greatness, whereas the Hope of Israel, the Lord Is Peace, the Father of Mercies, and the God of All Comfort convey the warmth and tenderness of a heavenly Father.

God's names are more than just titles to help you know who God is and what He's like. Within each of God's names comes an inherent promise: God can be relied on to be whatever His name says He is. While Mommy can get sick and not be able to be Mommy very well, or Sweetie can get angry and not be very sweet, or Ruth Ann Michaels can drop off the IRS rolls for one reason or another, "unlike them, [God] never changes" (James 1:17 NLT). God is always whatever His name says He is—*no matter what.*

So what's in a name? Plenty, when the name is God's. Look for the names of God whenever you read the Bible. See how they can be used in your life to help you grow in your faith. The book of Psalms is full of God's descriptive names, for the psalmist experienced God working in and through his life in many ways. Because God had always been steadfast and unmovable, the psalmist praised God as the Rock. Because God never sins or does anything wrong, the psalmist could call God the Holy One. In the same way, as you read through the Bible you can always trust God to be the Everlasting God, the Living God, and the One Who Sees You. You can always count on Him to be with you and to provide for you because He is also named I Am, the Lord Is There, and the Lord Will Provide. As you read through the Bible, the Mighty One, the Strength of Israel, assures you that He will be stronger than any situation you have to face. You'll find abundant reasons to praise your Lord and King when you count on Him to be whatever His name says He is.

God
What's in a Name?

What Matters Most...

- Knowing that God has many different names, just as people do.

- Understanding that each name used for God in Scripture reflects a different facet of His being and character.

- Remembering the promise within God's names: He can be relied on to be whatever His name says He is.

- Believing that God never changes—no matter what.

- Recognizing that the Bible is the best source to help you learn more about Him and the power of His name.

What Doesn't Matter...

- That you've never before noticed that God's names had significance or relevance to your daily life.

- That you're more familiar with wrestlers or penitentiaries known as the Rock than you are with God as your Rock of Ages.

- How many of God's names you know. As you read the Bible, you'll find out more about Him and see how God's names can impact your life.

- How many times you've failed to be what you've said you are: loving daughter, faithful friend, kind coworker.

Focus Points...

"I am the Alpha and the Omega—the beginning and the end," says the Lord God. "I am the one who is, who always was, and who is still to come, the Almighty One."
REVELATION 1:8 NLT

Anyone who is sick should call the church's elders. They should pray for and pour oil on the person in the name of the Lord.
JAMES 5:14 NCV

You must not use the name of the LORD your God thoughtlessly; the LORD will punish anyone who misuses his name.
EXODUS 20:7 NCV

Blessed be the name of the LORD from this time on and forevermore. From the rising of the sun to its setting the name of the LORD is to be praised.
PSALM 113:2–3 NRSV

what really counts

When you live on a faith basis, your desire will be only for that which you can ask in God's name.
NORMAN VINCENT PEALE

Jehovah, great I AM, by earth and heaven confessed: I bow and bless the sacred name forever blest.
THOMAS OLIVERS

God
Face-to-Face

The LORD spoke to Moses face to
face as a man speaks with his friend.
EXODUS 33:11 NCV

You do many things with your face on any given day. You may put creams on your wrinkles or makeup on your freckles. You may scowl in displeasure or smile with happiness. You may carry on a face-to-face conversation with a friend or turn your face away from someone to concentrate, cry, or sneeze. One thing is for sure: your face gets a workout on a daily basis.

According to the Bible, God does many things with His face too. When God wants to offer grace, help, or blessings in some way to His people, He turns His face toward them. The psalmist so trusted this aspect of God's character that he often prayed for God to "be gracious to us and bless us and make his face shine upon us" (Psalm 67:1 NIV). However, there are many times in the Bible when God was displeased or angry with His children. During those times, God said He would turn His face away from His people and show them

His back instead. For God to turn His face away from His people meant He would withhold His favor, grace, and blessing. Thankfully, the Bible promises that God won't stay angry with His children forever, but insists that God will turn His face of blessing toward all who return to Him.

Moses understood the favor found in the shining of God's face. While leading the Israelites to the Promised Land, Moses would often go by himself into the tent that the people used for worship. Whenever Moses entered this tabernacle, God would come in the pillar of cloud and talk with Moses "face to face, as a man speaks to his friend" (Exodus 33:11 NKJV). During those close encounters, Moses would find the direction and strength he needed to continue to lead God's people.

If you long for such a close relationship with God, why not add a little something to your daily facial workout? Give your spiritual face a chance for a daily face-to-face chat with God. Even without a tabernacle in your backyard, you can still humbly seek God's face in prayer. When you do, He has promised to listen, to forgive, and to heal. When you set your face to follow Him, you'll find His direction, mercy, and strength. Actively seek a face-to-face encounter with God. His blessing, grace, and favor are waiting for you.

God
Face-to-Face

What Matters Most...

◉ Trusting that God will be true to His character, that He will be gracious and good when His face shines on His children.

◉ Realizing that God often turns His face—His blessing, favor, and grace—away from His children when they disobey.

◉ Recognizing that even if you have wandered away from God, He will shine His face of blessing on you if you return to Him.

◉ Understanding that a close relationship with God can come only if you seek God's face on a regular basis.

What **Doesn't** Matter...

◉ Whether your face is wrinkled, freckled, scowling, or smiling.

◉ Whether you've ever sought God's face in prayer before now. It's never too late to begin to build a relationship with God through prayer.

◉ That you're not a Bible hero like Moses with a tabernacle in your backyard. You don't need to be a celebrity.

◉ Perfection. You'll displease God sometimes. You're human. But as you seek God's face, you'll grow closer to Him and also find that following Him becomes/is easier.

Focus Points...

When You said, "Seek My face," my heart said to You, "Your face, LORD, I will seek."
PSALM 27:8 NKJV

The LORD make his face shine upon you and be gracious to you; the LORD turn his face toward you and give you peace.
NUMBERS 6:25–26 NIV

If My people who are called by My name will humble them-selves, and pray and seek My face, and turn from their wicked ways, then I will hear from heaven.
2 CHRONICLES 7:14 NKJV

The eyes of the Lord are on the righteous, and his ears are open to their prayer. But the face of the Lord is against those who do evil.
1 PETER 3:12 NRSV

what really counts

Restore us, O God; make your face shine upon us, that we may be saved.
PSALM 80:3 NIV

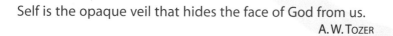

Self is the opaque veil that hides the face of God from us.
A. W. TOZER

The soul can split the sky in two and let the face of God shine through.
EDNA ST. VINCENT MILLAY

God
With a Wave

> I will teach you about the hand of God; what is with the Almighty I will not conceal.
>
> JOB 27:11 NKJV

what really counts

Elbow, elbow, wrist, wrist. These are the elements of the royal wave—that upward-raised arm, wrist-rotating hand motion that members of royalty use as they pass in review of their loyal subjects. With a wave of the hand the royals confer greeting and grace, recognition and response, power and prestige. When a royal personage waves his or her hand, sovereignty is acknowledged, whether the celebrated one is a British monarch or a high-school prom queen.

Just as the hand of an earthly monarch conveys power and authority with only a wave, so God's hand symbolizes His supreme sovereignty and power over everything on earth. The psalmist acknowledged that God created the world *with* His hand, holds the whole world *in* His hand, and *opens* His hand to feed "every living thing" on it (Psalm 145:16 NKJV). The ancient prophets proclaimed the mightiness of God's hand, announcing that God would bring about judgment through the power of His hand. With a wave of His hand, God would bring so much trouble on the ungodly that His enemies would "be afraid and fear because of the waving of the hand of the LORD of hosts" (Isaiah 19:16 NKJV).

The hand of God in Scripture also points to God's sovereignty in His actions on His people's behalf. Redemption and salvation come through God's powerful hand, ensuring success, victory, and strength for His people. God's hand inspired the prophets, too, and miraculously delivered the Israelites from slavery in Egypt. Because God's hand is invincible, He will fulfill all the plans and purposes He has set in motion. Therefore, as God's child, you can joyously submit to God's authority, knowing that His mighty hand will work out everything for your good.

So whenever you see the elbow-elbow-wrist-wrist royal wave of an earthly monarch, let it remind you of everything that God's hand means for you. He offers you His hand of mercy when you have fallen, His hand of compassion when you hurt. He holds you close in the palm of His hand, and His blessings pour forth from His bountiful hand. With a wave of His hand, He rules the world and grants you strength and victory over circumstances so that you can say with the psalmist, "I will sing for joy about what your hands have done" (Psalm 92:4 NCV). That's the power of God's hand.

God
With a Wave

What Matters Most...

◉ Seeing God's hand and remembering His supreme sovereignty over everything.

◉ Seeing God's hand and trusting in the promise of His care.

◉ Seeing God's hand and realizing the personal blessings available to you.

◉ Seeing God's hand and rejoicing in it. His hand pours out blessing after blessing. His care is never-ending.

What Doesn't Matter...

◉ That you've never before noticed the important lessons that the Bible teaches about God's hand. Start today. Read the Bible.

◉ That it's hard to sometimes see God's hand at work in your life. The pressures of life can cloud your spiritual focus. Ask God to clearly reveal His hand in your life.

◉ That you've never acknowledged God's hand at work in your life. You can always start now by praising God for your blessings.

◉ That you've seen God's hand only as a tool of judgment. God's hand holds blessing, compassion, mercy, grace, and forgiveness, too.

Focus Points...

He is our God, and we are the people of His pasture, and the sheep of His hand.
PSALM 95:7 NKJV

There is nothing better for people to do than to eat, drink, and find satisfaction in their work. I saw that even this comes from the hand of God.
ECCLESIASTES 2:24 GOD'S WORD

In His hand are the deep places of the earth; the heights of the hills are His also. The sea is His, for He made it; and His hands formed the dry land.
PSALM 95:4–5 NKJV

The righteous and the wise and their works are in the hand of God.
ECCLESIASTES 9:1 NKJV

what really counts

LORD, you are our Father. We are the clay, and you are the potter. We are all formed by your hand.
ISAIAH 64:8 NLT

I cannot, but God can; oh, balm for all my care! The burden that I drop His hand will lift and bear.
ANNIE JOHNSON FLINT

I have lived, seen God's hand thro' a lifetime, and all was for best.
ROBERT BROWNING

God
Timetables

Rest in the LORD, and wait
patiently for Him.

PSALM 37:7 NKJV

How well do you wait? You wait in traffic and in checkout lines. You wait for phone calls, for public transportation, for news about loved ones. You wait nine months to deliver a baby. And despite microwave technology, you even have to wait for supper. That five-minute wait for a TV dinner seems to take forever.

With all the waiting you already do, there's still an extra item to add to your waiting list: waiting for God. God's timetable for your life may not always agree with yours. You may be unsure about a direction or decision and find yourself waiting for His guidance. You may be facing a tight financial squeeze, waiting for the fulfillment of His promised provision. You may have been wronged and now wait for His justice. Or you may have wandered away from God's best for your life and now wait for His renewal of your spirit.

Waiting for God isn't easy, but it is essential to achieving a strong faith and a blessed life. King Saul found that out the hard way. Saul wasn't good at waiting, either. He had been fighting Israel's enemies in the hills outside Jerusalem. His troops were disheartened because the enemy had called up thirty thousand fresh charioteers. King Saul knew that Samuel the prophet was on his way to pray for God's intervention, but Saul had already been waiting for Samuel seven days. Now his troops were deserting him, so Saul wouldn't wait any longer. Even though he knew it was against God's law for him to offer sacrifices because he wasn't a priest, King Saul took matters into his own hands and offered the sacrifices himself. However, "just as he finished making the offering, Samuel arrived" (1 Samuel 13:10 NIV). Samuel was angry and told King Saul that he had been foolish, that the Lord would have established his kingdom if Saul had been obedient and waited, but now Saul's kingdom would come to an end.

Whenever you find yourself waiting for God's instructions, the fulfillment of His promises, His justice, or the renewal of your heart, remember the lesson of King Saul. Don't take matters into your own hands. Wait for God's timing, for the blessing hidden within the wait. God waited for you to come to faith in Him. Now it's your turn. "Wait, I say, on the LORD!" (Psalm 27:14 NKJV).

God
Timetables

What Matters Most...

◎ Knowing that even though waiting for God isn't easy, waiting is essential for achieving a strong faith and a blessed life.

◎ Remembering that impatience from within and pressure from without can make waiting for God extremely difficult.

◎ Understanding that God is always working on your behalf.

◎ Recognizing that God has waited for you—to come to faith in Him, to talk to Him about your needs. He waits for you; learn to wait for Him.

What Doesn't Matter...

◎ How fast you want things done. Your times are in God's hands. He is watching the timetable, and He has never been late yet.

◎ How long you have to wait. Wait until God moves, acts, or responds.

◎ How well you think you can handle the situation on your own. When you ask for God's help, wait for God's answer.

◎ Whether others desert you while you wait for God. Do things God's way; wait for Him.

Focus Points...

Wait on the LORD; be of good courage, and He shall strengthen your heart; wait, I say, on the LORD!
PSALM 27:14 NKJV

The LORD is waiting to be kind to you. He rises to have compassion on you. The LORD is a God of justice. Blessed are all those who wait for him.
ISAIAH 30:18 GOD'S WORD

I wait for the LORD, my soul waits, and in His word I do hope.
PSALM 130:5 NKJV

I waited patiently for the LORD; he turned to me and heard my cry.
PSALM 40:1 NIV

It is good to wait quietly for salvation from the LORD.
LAMENTATIONS 3:26 NLT

what really counts

Rest assured that if God waits longer than we desire, it is simply to make the blessings doubly precious.

ANDREW MURRAY

Waiting—keeping yourself faithful to His leading—this is the secret of strength. And anything that does not align with obedience to Him is a waste of time and energy. Watch and wait for His leading.

SAMUEL DICKEY GORDON

What Matters Most to Me About
God

What a great, big, wonderful God! Faithful to His promises, reliable to be what He says He will be. Wise enough to keep you waiting for His very best. Gracious enough to shine His face on you and pour His hand of blessings out on you. Glory God as you reflect on these thoughts.

◎ *Borrow a hymnbook from a church or library, and find a familiar song that talks about God's character and name. Knowing that God can be trusted to be whatever His name says, what does this hymn or song tell you about God and His interaction in your life? Record your observations.*

_____

_____

_____

_____

_____

_____

◎ *Remember a time when you had to wait for God to answer a prayer or solve a problem. What facets of God's hand can you now see in the way the prayer or problem was answered or resolved? List those reminders for future reference.*

_____

_____

_____

_____

_____

◎ *List every good thing you can think of in your life. Realizing that your blessings come from God's hand, take time to write a prayer of thanks for the good things God has given you.*

_____

_____

_____

_____

_____

_____

_____

_____

_____

◎ *Stand in front of the mirror and take a look at your face. Imagine God standing alongside you, with His face joining your reflection. Remember that God loves you, cares for you, and wants to help you be the best you can be. Record the feelings you have when seeing God face-to-face in this way.*

_____

_____

_____

_____

_____

_____

_____

_____

Don't get so absorbed and exhausted in taking care of all your day-by-day obligations that you lose track of the time and doze off, oblivious to God . . . Be up and awake to what God is doing!

ROMANS 13:11–12 MSG

GOD

JESUS

An Introduction

> You shall call His name JESUS, for He will save His people from their sins.
>
> MATTHEW 1:21 NKJV

what really counts

Pollsters indicate that while most people have heard *about* Jesus, very few claim a personal relationship with Him. Yet a personal relationship with Jesus is absolutely necessary if you wish to be relieved of the guilt of past mistakes and find contentment, peace, happiness, and satisfaction in life.

A close relationship with Jesus can come about only through a life-changing experience called salvation. Jesus' death on the cross makes the wonderful gift of salvation possible. This wonderful gift can remove anything that separates you from closeness with God and can transform your inner spirit into a heart full of His love. When your heart is transformed through the gift of salvation, God also makes you one of His children. That means that Jesus Christ, His Son, is your brother—the best big brother ever. And, because Jesus is the co-equal, co-eternal Son of God, He has been given all authority over everything in heaven and earth. This means Jesus is not only your Savior, He is also your Lord. He is to be the One who calls all the shots in your life. But that's okay too, because now you're family.

Don't forget that Jesus is also the best mentor you could ever wish for. Within the pages of the Bible, Jesus sets an example for all women in faithfulness, patience, self-denial, prayer, purity, and service to others. Don't be satisfied just knowing *about* Jesus. Get to know Him personally to experience a life that will glorify and please God.

> The greatest thing about any civilization is the human person, and the greatest thing about this person is the possibility of his encounter with the person of Jesus Christ.
>
> CHARLES MALIK

Jesus
A Gift for You

He saved us, not on the basis of deeds which we have done in righteousness, but according to His mercy.

TITUS 3:5 NASB

what really counts

A wide concrete stairway led up from the street. A sturdy handrail bordered one side of the steps. At the top of the stairway, a broad sidewalk swept across an expanse of lawn. The only problem with this entrance was its finishing point; the sidewalk ran directly into the side of a building. Though it was well maintained, the stairway and sidewalk led nowhere.

When it comes to changing their lives for the better, women can often be on a sidewalk to nowhere and not even realize it. Lasting inner change that brings about peace, happiness, and satisfaction in life involves transformation, and women try many different ways to transform themselves into better people. Addicts may go to group meetings; overweight ladies may try weight-loss clinics. Some try psychotherapy; others rely on meditation techniques. A few strong-willed women may purpose on their own to be good people at all times in all situations. Although these activities can change a physical or mental outlook on things, they are like the stairway and sidewalk that lead nowhere. Mental and physical adaptation techniques won't bring you the true transformation you seek. Why? Because these changes are only skindeep. To change your life for the better, you need a transformed heart.

Consider this: you've probably gotten angry, been self-centered, or in some other way done or said something contrary to what God wants. In the Bible, that contrariness is called sin. Sin keeps your heart stirred up, keeps you feeling anxious, guilty, or that something's missing in your life. God offers to remove those feelings and give you peace and joy instead. He offers you a gift—the Bible calls it salvation—through the death of His Son, Jesus, on the cross. When you believe that Jesus died on that cross to remove your contrariness and restore you to a full, loving relationship with God, your inner spirit is miraculously transformed. This transformation, this salvation of your spirit, is not the result of personal achievement, mental acuity, or good living. Salvation depends totally upon Jesus. Anything else is just a stairway and sidewalk to nowhere.

So for a true inner transformation, let Jesus be your Savior. He alone is the way to bring you back to an eternal relationship with God. Seek His forgiveness for your self-centeredness. And believe in Jesus' saving power to transform your heart, for "by believing in him, anyone can have a whole and lasting life" (John 3:16 MSG).

Jesus
A Gift for You

What Matters Most...

◎ Jesus. The power of His name can truly transform your inner spirit.

◎ Jesus. He alone provides the way for you to have a whole, glorious, and lasting life.

◎ Jesus. The transformation of your heart depends totally on Him and not on any mental or physical adaptation techniques you may ever try.

◎ Jesus. His sacrifice on the cross removes your sins and restores you to a loving relationship with God.

What **Doesn't** Matter...

◎ All the mental and physical adaptation techniques you could ever try. You might physically feel better, but your soul will still be sin-sick.

◎ Your mental acuity. Your intelligence quotient, test scores, or Mensa abilities won't transform your inner spirit. Salvation comes through Jesus alone.

◎ Your personal achievements in life. Personal achievements don't guarantee salvation. Only Jesus does.

◎ That it seems too simple. Simple things are usually the best—for life and spiritual transformation.

Focus Points...

We have seen and testify that the Father has sent his Son to be the Savior of the world.
1 JOHN 4:14 NIV

We ourselves have heard Him and we know that this is indeed the Christ, the Savior of the world.
JOHN 4:42 NKJV

If you confess with your mouth the Lord Jesus and believe in your heart that God has raised Him from the dead, you will be saved.
ROMANS 10:9 NKJV

God in his gracious kindness declares us not guilty. He has done this through Christ Jesus, who has freed us by taking away our sins.
ROMANS 3:24 NLT

what really counts

Most assuredly, I say to you, he who believes in Me has everlasting life.
JOHN 6:47 NKJV

Salvation is not something that is done for you but something that happens within you. It is not the clearing of a court record, but the transformation of a life attitude.

ALBERT W. PALMER

Jesus is not one of many ways to approach God, nor is He the best of several ways; He is the only way.

A. W. TOZER

Jesus
What Jesus Says, Goes

You call Me Teacher and Lord,
and you say well, for so I am.
JOHN 13:13 NKJV

It was Michelle's first day on the job. The new position meant learning new skills and adjusting to a new boss. Michelle knew that bosses and jobs just go together. Any time you take a position in a company, church, military, or civic organization, you'll always find someone in authority over you. The Bible indicates that there is always Someone in authority over you in spiritual things, too. That Someone is Jesus Christ.

The Bible uses the title Lord or Master to indicate Jesus' spiritual authority, calling Him the Lord of the Church and the Lord of the Sabbath. The Bible further expands Jesus' authority, declaring that He is Lord of All, that all authority has been given to Him by God, both "in heaven and on earth" (Matthew 28:18 NKJV). Because of His sacrifice for you on the cross, because He is the co-equal, co-eternal Son of God, and because He rules the angels and powers of earth at God's right side in heaven, what Jesus says, goes. In everything, Jesus is to take first place; He is to be the boss of everything and everyone.

So how does it work? How do you let Jesus be your divine boss, your Lord and spiritual authority? In the Bible, He has told you what He wants you to do, what priorities He wants you to set. To make Jesus the Lord of your life, do what He says. Show His love to others. Follow His directives. Tell others about the wonderful things He has done for you, about the transformation He's made of your inner spirit. Listen to what He says by reading the Bible, studying it, and applying the things you've learned. Through prayer, let Jesus point out areas of your life that need to be changed, and then ask Him to help you change them.

Though earthly bosses may exercise their authority in harsh ways, you'll never have to dread working for your spiritual boss, your heavenly Lord and Master. His power as sovereign Lord is an awesome thing, yet the Bible reassures you that Jesus' lordship of your life is something to be valued, not feared. When you submit to His authority, when you follow His direction for your life, He promises you a special relationship with Him that is full of grace, mercy, peace, and joy. Ask Jesus to be Lord of your life. Remember, He wants only what's best for you.

Jesus
What Jesus Says, Goes

What Matters Most...

◎ Remembering that there will always be someone in authority over you, whether you're working here on earth or dealing with spiritual matters.

◎ Remembering that God has given all authority in heaven and on earth to Jesus. He is your spiritual authority, your heavenly Master, your Lord.

◎ Remembering that Jesus is the co-equal, co-eternal Son of God, and what He says, goes.

◎ Remembering that when you ask Jesus to be the Lord of your life, you will gain a special relationship with Him that is marked by grace, mercy, peace, and joy.

What **Doesn't** Matter...

◎ The dread you feel over facing a new boss. You don't have to fear Jesus. He has your best interests at heart.

◎ How many times a boss at work has mistreated you or overlooked you. Human bosses are fallible. Jesus isn't.

◎ That serving someone doesn't sound like much fun. Jesus wants you to be His hands, His heart, and to bring His love to others.

◎ Your unfamiliarity with what Jesus wants you to do. Read Matthew or Mark in the Bible. Look for Jesus' words.

Focus Points...

At the name of Jesus every knee should bow, of those in heaven, and of those on earth, and of those under the earth, and that every tongue should confess that Jesus Christ is Lord, to the glory of God the Father.
PHILIPPIANS 2:10–11 NKJV

There is only one Lord, Jesus Christ, through whom God made everything and through whom we have been given life.
1 CORINTHIANS 8:6 NLT

God has put all things under the authority of Christ, and he gave him this authority for the benefit of the church.
EPHESIANS 1:22 NLT

Just as you accepted Christ Jesus as your Lord, you must continue to live in obedience to him.
COLOSSIANS 2:6 NLT

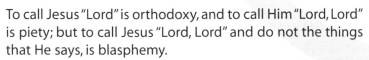

To call Jesus "Lord" is orthodoxy, and to call Him "Lord, Lord" is piety; but to call Jesus "Lord, Lord" and do not the things that He says, is blasphemy.

LESLIE WEATHERHEAD

Jesus Christ will be Lord of all or he will not be Lord at all.

SAINT AUGUSTINE

Jesus
A Super Sibling

> If we are God's children, we will receive blessings from God together with Christ.
>
> ROMANS 8:17 NCV

Did you have a brother at home when you were growing up? Little brothers could be a nuisance, tagging along when unwanted, spying on you when you'd least expect it, and tattling about everything to everyone. Big brothers often weren't much better. They'd often pick on you, bully the guys who'd want to date you, and use their size and age to their advantage to get the car first, the remote control first, and all the leftovers in the fridge, too. Brothers.

Big brothers in the Bible weren't always the most helpful to their sisters, either. Though God's law said that physical brothers were to protect a sister at all times, watch over the details of her marriage, and take care of the hard things for her like a parent's death, some biblical big brothers like Simeon, Levi, and Absalom used their muscles instead of their hearts, falling short of their responsibilities and failing their sisters. However, there is one big brother mentioned in the Bible who never fails in His care for His sisters. That super sibling is Jesus.

Think of it this way. Because all believers are collectively the children of one heavenly Father, you are related to God's Son, Jesus. Not only is Jesus your Savior, He's your spiritual big brother, too, a sibling like no other. With Jesus standing in as your spiritual big brother, you can rely on Him to take care of the hard things in your life. He can be your strong shoulder when things go wrong, or the One you run to with good news. You don't have to be afraid, either, because as your spiritual brother, Jesus will watch out for you and care for you always.

Because of your faith in Jesus, you are also His spiritual sister. That means you have all the rights and privileges of being God's child. You are a co-heir with Jesus, you can share in God's work together, and you can have a close relationship with God the Father *and* your big brother, Jesus. So spend some time with Jesus in prayer. Trust Him to be the big brother you've always wanted. And be His true sister, too. Live your life the way God wants you to live, for your heavenly brother once proclaimed, "My true brother and sister and mother are those who do what God wants" (Mark 3:35 NCV).

Jesus
A Super Sibling

What Matters Most...

- Recognizing that God wants brothers to care for their sisters.

- Remembering that as a child of God, you are related to His Son, Jesus. Jesus is your spiritual big brother.

- Believing that with Jesus as your heavenly big brother, you can rely on Him.

- Understanding that as Jesus' sister, you have all the rights and privileges of one of God's children.

What **Doesn't** Matter...

- How many earthly siblings you do or don't have. As a child of God, you have a spiritual family, and a loving, caring, big brother.

- What your relationship has been like with your physical kinfolk. Good or bad, they're still your relatives.

- What you are going through right now. God wanted big brothers to help their sisters during tough times.

- The depth of your Christian faith. You'll grow in your faith as you get to know Him better.

- What others say about you. Jesus' opinion is what counts.

Focus Points...

Behold what manner of love the Father has bestowed on us, that we should be called children of God!
1 JOHN 3:1 NKJV

God knew his people in advance, and he chose them to become like his Son, so that his Son would be the firstborn, with many brothers and sisters.
ROMANS 8:29 NLT

Jesus, who makes people holy, and those who are made holy are from the same family. So he is not ashamed to call them his brothers and sisters.
HEBREWS 2:11 NCV

As many as received Him, to them He gave the right to become children of God, to those who believe in His name.
JOHN 1:12 NKJV

what really counts

I'm so glad I'm a part of the family of God—I've been washed in the fountain, cleansed by His blood! Joint heirs with Jesus as we travel this sod; for I'm part of the family, the family of God.

WILLIAM J. GAITHER

Christ is full and sufficient for all his people ... a Husband to protect; a Father to provide; a Brother to relieve; a Foundation to support.

JOHN SPENCER

Jesus
Follow Me

Follow my example, as I follow
the example of Christ.
1 Corinthians 11:1 ncv

Can you remember your first day on your first job? Maybe you were a teenager babysitting for a neighbor. Maybe you worked at a fast-food restaurant, or delivered newspapers or pizzas or telephone books. Whatever your first job, you probably were unsure about an aspect of the work or the uniform or the time card. By watching coworkers or your boss, you probably learned a lot. Hopefully their examples were good ones, for following a good example would help you succeed in your work.

For building a strong Christian faith there's no better example to follow than that of Jesus Christ. One day Jesus and His disciples were walking near Caesarea Philippi in the northeastern corner of Palestine. A crowd of people began to follow them as they walked and talked together, until Jesus finally stopped and addressed the crowd. "'If any of you wants to be my follower,' he told them, 'you must put aside your self-

58

ish ambition, shoulder your cross, and follow me'" (Mark 8:34 NLT).

Can you picture it? Grandmas and grandpas, moms with babies on their hips or tots held by the hand, men on their way to or from business—all gathered around Jesus, all given the same message: "Follow Me." Heretofore that message had been reserved for only the disciples, but then Jesus extended His call to women, children, old, and young. Follow Me, Jesus said, and I will show you how to grow up spiritually. Follow My example to learn self-denial, faithfulness, and patience. Follow Me to learn to pray, to love, and to serve others. Follow My example, and you'll be more like Me every day.

This is Jesus' message for you, too. Jesus calls you to follow His example in the way you interact with others, in how you do your work, in where you place your priorities. Every time you're unsure about a decision, search the Bible to see what Jesus did to make wise choices. Whenever someone hurts your feelings or ridicules you for your faith, let Jesus' example help you respond as He did: "I have given you an example, that you should do as I have done" (John 13:15 NKJV). There is a caveat and reward in Jesus' message too: "If you understand what I'm telling you, act like it—and live a blessed life" (John 13:17 MSG).

Jesus
Follow Me

What Matters Most...

◎ Knowing that Jesus has called you, a woman in the twenty-first century, to follow His example in your daily life.

◎ Realizing that following Jesus' example applies to all areas of your life—your relationships, your home, your family, and your work.

◎ Remembering that the Bible is the source for finding out about Jesus' life and the example for your life.

◎ Recognizing that following Jesus' example can bring about a blessed life.

What **Doesn't** Matter...

◎ That you're not very good at telling good examples from bad ones. Just remember that Jesus is your best example.

◎ Whether you're unsure of what direction to go, what decision to make, or what friends to choose. Jesus' example found in the Bible can help you make wise choices.

◎ Whether you're old or young, employed or not, single or married.

◎ Your ambitions. If you truly want to be a follower of Jesus, self-denial, patience, love, and service are hallmarks of His example for you to follow.

◎ Merely reading about Jesus and His life. Follow Jesus' example.

Focus Points...

Calling the crowd to join his disciples, he said, "Anyone who intends to come with me has to let me lead. You're not in the driver's seat; I am ... Follow me."
MARK 8:34 MSG

Whoever serves me must follow me. Then my servant will be with me everywhere I am.
JOHN 12:26 NCV

My sheep hear My voice, and I know them, and they follow Me.
JOHN 10:27 NKJV

Live a life filled with love for others, following the example of Christ, who loved you and gave himself as a sacrifice to take away your sins.
EPHESIANS 5:2 NLT

what really counts

Jesus did not say, "Come to me and get it over with." He said, "If any man would come after me, let him take up his cross daily and follow me." *Daily* is the key word.
LOUIS CASSELS

Follow me; I am the way, the truth, and the life. Without the way there is no going; without the truth there is no knowing; without the life there is no living.
THOMAS À KEMPIS

What Matters Most to Me About
Jesus

Savior. Lord. Brother. Example. Jesus is everything you'll ever need to live a life that's pleasing to God. Contemplate the fullness of faith you receive through Him as you respond to these thoughts.

◎ *Take a moment and think back to the day when you first became aware of everything Jesus did for you on the cross. Record those impressions here. How has having Jesus as your Savior changed your life inwardly and outwardly?*

_____

_____

_____

_____

_____

_____

_____

◎ *Make a list of traits a good boss would possess. Alongside that list, record how Jesus personifies those traits. At the bottom of the list, compose a prayer committing your heart to serve willingly under Jesus' leadership and lordship.*

_____

_____

_____

_____

_____

_____

Write a brief prayer to thank Jesus for being your big brother. Then choose one of the verses from the previous pages that speak about being family together with Jesus and rewrite it here, personalizing it with your name. Allow the knowledge that Jesus cares for you as family give you confidence, strength, and hope as you go through the days ahead.

_____

_____

_____

_____

_____

_____

_____

List two or three names of people close to you who need to hear about Jesus as Savior and Lord. Brainstorm here a few ways to share your faith story with them so that they, too, can hear Jesus' call to "follow Me."

_____

_____

_____

_____

_____

_____

_____

_____

God so loved the world that He gave His only begotten Son, that whoever believes in Him should not perish but have everlasting life. For God did not send His Son into the world to condemn the world, but that the world through Him might be saved.

JOHN 3:16–17 NKJV

THE HOLY SPIRIT

An Introduction

> He breathed on them, and said to them, "Receive the Holy Spirit."
>
> JOHN 20:22 NKJV

what really counts

The early church drafted a mission statement called the Nicene Creed to help solidify the core beliefs of the Christian faith. This creed contains a brief description of "the Lord, the giver of life," that was meant to teach believers more about the eternal Holy Spirit of God, His co-equal status with the Father and the Son, and His ministry, both in the world and with God's children. Even today, learning such facts about the Holy Spirit can strengthen your faith and help you understand how God's Holy Spirit works in and through people and situations.

Yet facts can be limiting. Even if you know all the facts about a person, it is only when you interact with someone and get to know them on a more personal level that you really begin to grow in your relationship with them. For you to grow in your relationship with God's Holy Spirit, you need to get to know Him in a more personal way, too, to understand the ways in which He impacts your life. For example, some of the things that may be easy for you to do—helping, comforting, sharing, teaching, guiding—are all facets of the Holy Spirit Himself. When you ask God to let these traits blossom in your life, God can use you as His channel of blessing and mercy to others.

The Giver of Life longs to bless you, fill you, and use you for God's glory. Learn about the Holy Spirit. Grow in your relationship with Him. Get to know God in all His fullness.

> Whenever in any period of the history of the church a little company has sprung up so surrendered to the Holy Spirit, and so filled with His presence as to furnish the pliant instrument of His will, a new Pentecost has dawned on Christendom.
>
> A. J. GORDON

The Holy Spirit

God's Softer Side

> When He, the Spirit of truth, has come, He will guide you into all truth.
>
> JOHN 16:13 NKJV

what really counts

The Bible is a treasury of information about Him. Within its pages you can find out about God the Father—Creator, Judge, and Sovereign over everything. You can familiarize yourself with God's Son, Jesus—His life, teachings, sacrificial death, and resurrection. You can also see the softer side of God through the work and ministry of God's Holy Spirit.

Bible scholars have noted that wherever the Holy Spirit is mentioned in Scripture, He is spoken of in terms of gentleness and caring. Though the Bible records that both God the Father and God the Son display anger at times, you will never find a biblical reference to anger and God's Holy Spirit. Rather, Scripture illustrates the Holy Spirit's power, performance, and presence in the world through His gentle, compassionate care. The co-equal, co-eternal Spirit of God the Father and Son is often portrayed as a gentle "breath," "life," or "wind," illustrating His role in bringing new life to God's people. God's Spirit was an essential part of the earliest moments of creation, hovering over the land and water, giving life there, too. The Spirit also empowered the Old Testament judges to guide God's people and deliver them from oppression. And the Holy Spirit will empower the Messiah, too, by giving Him wisdom, understanding, counsel, might, and knowledge.

In the New Testament, the ministry of the Holy Spirit expands. His power is seen in the conception and birth of Jesus, the empowering of Jesus' teaching and ministry, and in Jesus' resurrection. The Spirit's presence brings blessing and fellowship to the early church, a sense of freedom and peace to troubled souls, and a source of teaching, comfort, counsel, and encouragement for the disciples as they take the gospel into the world.

Yet the Holy Spirit's role extends beyond the pages of the Bible. He is your perfect role model for being a Christian woman, too. The work and ministry that God's Holy Spirit performs as helper, comforter, encourager, and counselor are things that seem to come naturally to women, flowing from their lives without much effort. In essence, God has given women the image of His Holy Spirit so that His love can pour through you, through the power of His Spirit, and touch the lives of others. God's Holy Spirit is powerful, at work, and present within you. Let Him guide you as you grow to become the woman God has created you to be.

The Holy Spirit
God's Softer Side

What Matters Most...

◎ Remembering that the Holy Spirit is God; He is powerful, present, and at work in the world.

◎ Recognizing that the Holy Spirit is the source of the gentle things of God: comfort, encouragement, fellowship, and freedom.

◎ Understanding that the Holy Spirit can empower you for life and ministry.

◎ Realizing it's wonderful to be a woman, to be a natural channel for God's Holy Spirit to flow through you to others.

What **Doesn't** Matter...

◎ How much you know about God's Holy Spirit. The Bible is your guidebook to find out more.

◎ Your feelings of inadequacy. Don't worry. Let the Holy Spirit help you do whatever He guides you to do.

◎ Your perception that the Holy Spirit can use others more than you. God knows you and your abilities.

◎ Your social or economic standing. Money or status is not important to God's Spirit; willingness to be used is.

Focus Points...

Repent, and let every one of you be baptized in the name of Jesus Christ for the remission of sins; and you shall receive the gift of the Holy Spirit.
ACTS 2:38 NKJV

Having believed, you were marked in him with a seal, the promised Holy Spirit.
EPHESIANS 1:13 NIV

When you are arrested and judged, don't worry ahead of time about what you should say. Say whatever is given you to say at that time, because it will not really be you speaking; it will be the Holy Spirit.
MARK 13:11 NCV

I will ask the Father, and he will give you another Counselor, who will never leave you. He is the Holy Spirit, who leads into all truth.
JOHN 14:16–17 NLT

The Holy Spirit is the divine substitute on earth today for the bodily presence of the Lord Jesus Christ two thousand years ago.

ALAN REDPATH

When we rely upon education, we get what education can do. When we rely upon eloquence, we get what eloquence can do. When we rely on the Holy Spirit, we get what God can do.

A. C. DIXON

The Holy Spirit

Wired for Life

He will give you mighty inner
strength through his Holy Spirit.
EPHESIANS 3:16 NLT

what really counts

If you've ever watched new homes being built, you've probably seen workers running electrical lines to the rooms in each home. Wires tie junction boxes, fuse panels, and outlets together so that when the lines are connected to the main electrical supply, power can flow and lightbulbs can light up.

In a similar way, your inner spirit is like one of those homes; God's Holy Spirit is like the electrical wiring, supplying power to every part of your spirit. However, instead of being able to illuminate lightbulbs, when you have a close relationship with God, His Spirit wires you for living. His Spirit inhabits your being and can flow through you to others.

You won't find outlet boxes in your heart to prove God's Holy Spirit resides within you. Rather, when the Holy Spirit is your power source, you can sense inward changes in your heart and life. The Holy Spirit helps you live in unity with other believers and guards you from wickedness. The abiding sense that you are born anew, that you are God's child, that God lives in you, and that He is working through you are assurances that come from God's Holy Spirit within you. Your heartfelt concern for others, your ability to share your faith, to praise and worship God, to pray for others, to teach someone a truth from the Bible—all are confirmations of God's Spirit at work in you. Manifestations of God's Holy Spirit in you even include the sense that you've failed God and need forgiveness, your awareness of what decision to make in a challenging time, and your sense of well-being and peace.

Being wired for service isn't enough, however. Though new homes are wired for electrical service, occupants of these homes could stumble around in the dark if they never flip the switches and allow the electricity to flow. In the same way, you can be wired with God's Holy Spirit, but never sense, feel, or do any of the things the Holy Spirit is capable of doing in and through you. You need to flip the switch in your spirit to the On position by prayerfully asking God's Holy Spirit to flow through you and use you for His purposes. As a child of God, you are already wired for life; just let God's power flow from His Spirit through yours to change your life and the lives of others.

The Holy Spirit

Wired for Life

What Matters Most...

- ◎ Accepting the truth that God's Holy Spirit lives in His children and can work through each one.

- ◎ Realizing that the Holy Spirit's presence in your heart can affect your faith, decisions, and interactions with others.

- ◎ Recognizing that you can inhibit the Holy Spirit by refusing to let His power flow through you.

- ◎ Being willing to let God's power flow from His Spirit through yours to change your life and the lives of others.

What **Doesn't** Matter...

- ◎ Your age, sex, or shoe size. God fills all His children with His Spirit, empowering each one to be His channel of blessing.

- ◎ Your talents. Being filled with the Holy Spirit doesn't require a special talent, just a willing heart.

- ◎ Your church background. God's Spirit can work in anyone regardless of church affiliation.

- ◎ Your physical limitations. God's Spirit can empower anyone to sense, feel, or do God's work, despite health or physical limitations.

Focus Points...

The Spirit Himself bears witness with our spirit that we are children of God.
ROMANS 8:16 NKJV

The love of God has been poured out in our hearts by the Holy Spirit who was given to us.
ROMANS 5:5 NKJV

The Spirit of God whets our appetite by giving us a taste of what's ahead. He puts a little of heaven in our hearts so that we'll never settle for less.
2 CORINTHIANS 5:5 MSG

The Holy Spirit, whom the Father will send in My name, He will teach you all things, and bring to your remembrance all things that I said to you.
JOHN 14:26 NKJV

what really counts

Though every believer has the Holy Spirit, the Holy Spirit does not have every believer.

A. W. TOZER

Whether we preach, pray, write, do business, travel, take care of children or administer the government—whatever we do—our whole life and influence should be filled with the power of the Holy Spirit.

CHARLES G. FINNEY

What Matters Most to Me About
The Holy Spirit

To solidify in your heart what matters most to you about who
the Holy Spirit is and what He can do through you, journal your
responses to the statements below.

◎ *Reflect on ways that you have followed the Holy Spirit's work of bringing light
to darkness, life to barrenness, order to chaos. (Maybe you planted a garden in
a vacant lot, brightened a friend's dark day, or straightened a messy house.)
Thank God for opening your eyes to see these common tasks in new ways—as
manifestations of His Spirit working through you.*

_____

_____

_____

_____

_____

_____

◎ *When you are filled with the Holy Spirit, His characteristics can flow from
your life to others. Record here some of the ways that the Holy Spirit has used
you to show His traits of love, joy, peace, patience, kindness, goodness, faithfulness, gentleness, and self-control.*

_____

_____

_____

_____

_____

○ *The Holy Spirit was the power source for the Old Testament judges as they guided God's people. He will also empower the Messiah with wisdom, understanding, counsel, might, and knowledge. How has the Holy Spirit empowered you in these ways? Ask God to bring circumstances to mind, and record your thoughts here.*

_____

_____

_____

_____

_____

_____

_____

_____

○ *Choose two or three of the verses listed in the preceding meditations that describe a facet of the Holy Spirit that you would like to exhibit, sense, or see evidenced in your life. What must you do, change, or open your heart to in your life to make these things a reality?*

_____

_____

_____

_____

_____

_____

_____

_____

The Spirit is God's guarantee that he will give us everything he promised and that he has purchased us to be his own people. This is just one more reason for us to praise our glorious God.

EPHESIANS 1:14 NLT

FAITH

An Introduction

> The righteous will live by their faith.
>
> HABAKKUK 2:4 NLT

what really counts

Step through a door, flip a switch, and light floods the room. Turn a key in the ignition, and your car roars to life. Pop a cake into the oven, and in minutes you have a yummy dessert. All these commonplace activities are visual aids to faith.

Experience has taught you if you flip a switch you'll get light, if you turn a key you'll get ignition, or if you wait you'll get a cake when the timer dings. But faith takes you beyond your experience. Faith recognizes that things can go wrong—bulbs burn out, ignition coils can be faulty, recipe ingredients can be missing. Your inner outlook of faith, however, lets you put your full confidence in these things, assuring you all will be well—the lamp will light, the car will start, and the cake will be yummy like always.

Faith is more than experience, more than something you can see, taste, feel, or sense. Faith is a gift from God to your heart. Your faith—that belief, trust, and total confidence—in God and in His promises to you can be stronger than your faith in a lightbulb, auto ignition, or fresh-baked cake. He can remove any of your doubts if you pray and ask for a stronger faith. And if you've been hurt by someone who has violated your faith and trust, God can help you with that, too, for He is always trustworthy. In God you can find all the faith you need.

Life has dimensions other than those that can be encompassed by the sense, and into those dimensions nothing can enter except the principle of faith.

G. CAMPBELL MORGAN

Faith
I Believe!

Jesus answered and said to them, "Have faith in God."

MARK 11:22 NKJV

what really counts

In the Christmas classic *Miracle on 34th Street*, little Susie is haunted by doubts. Heading home from a Christmas party she absentmindedly repeats, "I believe . . . I believe" to bolster her faith in Santa Claus. The Hollywood ending to this tale intimates that you can find faith by ceaselessly repeating the right words. Unfortunately, that assumption is faulty. Faith isn't something you can work up by mouthing a mantra. Faith is a God-given gift.

According to the Bible, faith is not something you can see, touch, or use your senses to find. It's not something you can learn through prolonged study, nor is it an emotion or feeling. Rather, faith is a gift given by God in response to a heartfelt prayer of need, trust, or relinquishment. God-given faith has a childlike simplicity that willingly trusts, even when you can't see what lies ahead.

While some things may be easy to accept on faith—like believing some makeup and a curling iron will make you look younger—dealing with spiritual issues and practical problems can put faith to the test. A father once brought his demon-possessed son to Jesus, begging Him to heal the troubled boy. Jesus asked the man if he had faith that God could really help his son. "The father of the child cried out and said with tears, 'Lord, I believe; help my unbelief!'" (Mark 9:24 NKJV). The father wasn't just pretending to have faith like little Susie. Instead, he was being honest. He believed to a point, but there were doubts lurking in his heart, so he cried out for help. Jesus responded immediately, healing the son *and* increasing the father's faith.

When you plop yourself into a kitchen chair without a thought, you have faith that the chair will hold you. Experience has proved the chair is reliable. Your consistent use of that chair brings greater faith in its ability to hold you. This same principle applies to faith in God. Though God is more trustworthy than a kitchen chair, dropping your concerns on Him and believing that He will take care of them can be difficult at first. So be honest and say, "Lord, I believe; help my unbelief!" Because God promises to provide for, heal, give direction to, and care for you, the more consistent you are in asking for His help, the more you will experience His trustworthiness and the more your faith in Him will grow.

Faith
I Believe!

What Matters Most...

◉ Understanding that faith doesn't come from works, words, or worldly wisdom. Faith is a heart thing that comes from God.

◉ Remembering that doubt often lurks in the background whenever faith is being stretched. Show doubt the way out by asking God to help your unbelief.

◉ Learning to rely on faith in God for everything.

◉ Being honest with God about your faith, your unbelief, and your need for His help. God knows everything anyway, so be honest. Ask for His help to grow your faith.

What Doesn't Matter...

◉ That you don't believe in many things. Life's realities can harden a heart. God offers to soften hard hearts. Give Him a chance. Ask Him to grow your faith.

◉ That you have more faith in God's doing things for others than in His doing things for you. God doesn't play favorites. Have faith in Him to do what He says He will do for you.

◉ That you have only a little bit of faith. Even tiny faith, as small as a seed, can move an entire mountain of troubles. Have faith in God; He'll do the mountain-moving.

Focus Points...

We do not look at the things which are seen, but at the things which are not seen. For the things which are seen are temporary, but the things which are not seen are eternal ... For we walk by faith, not by sight.
2 CORINTHIANS 4:18; 5:7 NKJV

What is faith? It is the confident assurance that what we hope for is going to happen. It is the evidence of things we cannot yet see.
HEBREWS 11:1 NLT

Faith comes by hearing, and hearing by the word of God.
ROMANS 10:17 NKJV

If you do not stand firm in your faith, you will not stand at all.
ISAIAH 7:9 NIV

what really counts

Faith cannot be intellectually defined; faith is the inborn capacity to see God behind everything, the wonder that keeps you an eternal child.

OSWALD CHAMBERS

Faith is the power of putting self aside that God may work unhindered.

F. B. MEYER

81

Faith
Trust Me

Trust in the LORD forever, for the
LORD, the LORD, is the Rock eternal.
ISAIAH 26:4 NIV

The situation looks bleak. The hero—Aladdin, Luke Skywalker, Indiana Jones, or whoever—turns his face to the frightened heroine and boldly says, "Trust me!" before grasping the young maiden and leaping to safety . . . well, most of the time. Unfortunately, the hero and heroine can also jump into a worse situation—a pit of snakes, a rat-infested sewer, or right into the villain's grasp.

What Hollywood does for effect on film often happens in life as well. Someone says, "Trust me!" and when you do, you can end up in a worse mess than before. Yet there is Someone who is totally faithful, Someone in whom you can trust and never be disappointed. That Someone is God. And women have trusted Him for centuries.

Women of faith abound in the Bible: Rahab, who trusted God and two spies to gain salvation for her family; Deborah, who trusted God to give her wisdom to lead a nation; Ruth, whose newfound trust in God brought about a new marriage; Esther, who trusted her life to God and saved her people; and Mary, who trusted God's words and gave birth to a Savior. Yes, there are men in the Bible who exhibited faith (Shadrach, Meshach, and Abednego, for example) *and* women who were faithless (Eve, Jezebel, and Athaliah come to mind), but trust seems to come more easily to women. Researchers say that's how we're made.

And there's the rub, for where trust is, hurt sometimes follows. You've probably trusted people to do something they said they'd do, only to find they didn't do it. When this happens, trusting again is difficult. Yet God will *never* violate your trust. He is the hero whose hand you can clasp, knowing you'll never be disillusioned, never be let down, never be left alone. Faithfulness and trustworthiness are integral parts of His nature. God plans, and it is accomplished. God speaks, and it happens. God promises, and everything He says He will do, He does.

God is *faithful*. You can have faith in His love. You can trust Him to shower you with His power and strength. You can have faith in His unshakable salvation. When God says, "Trust Me!" you can place your faith in Him and leap into perfect peace, protection, strength, and freedom from fear. For a faith that trusts and is never disappointed, place your hand in the hand of a heavenly hero. Place your trust in God.

Faith
Trust Me

What Matters Most...

◎ Knowing there is Someone who is totally faithful, Someone in whom you can trust and never be disappointed. That Someone is God.

◎ Realizing that many of the heroes in the Bible were untrustworthy or faithless at times. People aren't perfect. People will be untrustworthy. But God won't.

◎ Knowing that trusting can be difficult after you've been hurt by someone untrustworthy. Yet God will never fail you. What He promises, He will do.

◎ Believing God is worthy of your full and total trust.

What Doesn't Matter...

◎ Who your heroes or heroines are. Fictional or real, larger than life or ordinary folks, human heroes and heroines have shortcomings. God doesn't.

◎ People who have failed you in their trustworthiness. Human beings are fallible. God isn't.

◎ How faithful you have or haven't been. God remains faithful even when you aren't. He never stops loving, caring for, forgiving, providing, or fulfilling His promises.

◎ How fearful you are to trust anyone completely. Total trust is tough if your trust has been broken before. Ask God to help you trust Him completely; receive His peace in return.

Focus Points...

You will keep in perfect peace all who trust in you, whose thoughts are fixed on you!
ISAIAH 26:3 NLT

Those who know Your name will put their trust in You; for You, LORD, have not forsaken those who seek You.
PSALM 9:10 NKJV

Trust in the LORD with all your heart, and lean not on your own understanding; in all your ways acknowledge Him, and He shall direct your paths.
PROVERBS 3:5–6 NKJV

Trust in Him at all times, O people; pour out your heart before Him; God is a refuge for us.
PSALM 62:8 NASB

what really counts

The LORD is good, a refuge in times of trouble. He cares for those who trust in him.
NAHUM 1:7 NIV

If the blind put their hand in God's, they find their way more surely than those who see but have not faith or purpose.
HELEN KELLER

We have heard of many people who trusted God too little, but have you ever heard of anyone who trusted Him too much?
J. HUDSON TAYLOR

What Matters Most to Me About
Faith

Your doubts and lack of trust can keep God from bringing wonderful blessings into your life. Journal your responses to the thoughts below as you seek to strengthen your faith in Him.

◎ *Take some time to think about the gift of faith that God offers you. Compose a prayer that both praises God for this gift and also petitions Him for a better understanding of faith and its work in your heart and life. Leave a space to record, at a later date, God's answer to your prayer.*

_____

_____

_____

_____

_____

_____

_____

◎ *The demon-possessed boy in the Bible benefited from his father's faith. You've probably been blessed in many ways through family traditions, personal experiences, and choices you've made. Record here how your faith is more than just another intellectual choice or ongoing family tradition.*

_____

_____

_____

_____

_____

_____

what
really
counts

◎ *Your salvation—your heart's transformation—is a gift from God. Because faith is a heart-gift that also comes from God, how do you see your faith and salvation working together? How should other God-given gifts—your talents and abilities, mercy, forgiveness, etc.—interact with your faith?*

_____

_____

_____

_____

_____

_____

_____

_____

◎ *The Bible assures you that God cares for all who put their trust in Him. What does this tell you about your faith and trust? In what ways have you found God to be trustworthy? How do these recollections give you peace, confidence, and hope?*

_____

_____

_____

_____

_____

_____

_____

_____

FAITH

This is the victory that has overcome the world—our faith.

1 JOHN 5:4 NKJV

LOVE

An Introduction

> If I speak with the tongues of men and of angels, but do not have love, I have become a noisy gong or a clanging cymbal.
>
> 1 CORINTHIANS 13:1 NASB

what really counts

Decades ago, a study in an orphanage in the former Soviet Union proved unequivocally that human beings need love. In a rather bizarre and cruel experiment, half of the infants in the orphanage's nursery received cuddling, kisses, and love from their caretakers. The remaining infants received only the rudimentary care of diaper changings and feedings. In a few months, the loved babies grew strong and thrived, yet the uncuddled, unkissed, unloved infants began to show signs of major illness.

The Soviet researchers learned through this experiment what moms the world over have known for centuries and what John Lennon penned in his 1960s pop tune: "All you need is love." God has created all people with a need to be loved. Yet only God offers an unconditional love that lets you be the real you that you are deep down inside. To receive God's love, you don't have to be, act, or do something special. God loves you just as you are. And, because of His love, you are free to become the person He created you to be.

Within the freedom found in God's love, there is also a hidden outcome—the ability to share that love with others. While the uncuddled Soviet orphans experienced the loneliness of a life deprived of love, God's love, flowing through you to another person, can help relieve another's loneliness and thereby help that person thrive and grow strong. Truly, then, all anyone needs is love.

> To know that we are loved by an omnipotent, omnipresent, omniscient Lord is the grandest feeling of acceptance anyone can have.
> THELMA WELLS

Love
Real Love

We love, because He first loved us.

1 JOHN 4:19 NASB

what really counts

In Margery Williams's timeless tale of *The Velveteen Rabbit*, a young boy receives a stuffed bunny as a gift. The bunny lives in the boy's room, waiting with the other toys to become the boy's playmate. A toy horse informs the velveteen rabbit that when a child loves a toy for a long, long time, something magical happens. Even though the toy may look worn and shabby to others, those things don't matter at all. A child's love goes deeper than the surface, overlooking the flaws and faults, ultimately transforming the toy so that it becomes "real."

Margery Williams understood the power of transforming love, and though her tale is pure fiction, there is a love that is great enough to transform a life. That love is God's love. God's love touched a man named Paul and transformed him from a persecutor of Christians to one of the church's greatest evangelists. God's love touched a woman who had been hemorrhaging for twelve years and transformed her into a vital, healthy family member. God's love touched a heart-broken, barren wife named Hannah and transformed her into a joyful new mom.

God's love can transform you, too. When God's love is at work in you, you know for sure that you are His child, that He is working out everything for your good. When God's love fills your heart, your days resonate with peace and joy. God's love molds your spirit, too, making you more like Himself, giving "you a new heart with new and right desires" (Ezekiel 36:26 NLT). But more than that, God's love can give you what the velveteen rabbit longed for. God's love can free you to become "real." Because His love is so much deeper than human love, you don't have to pretend with Him. You can be yourself when you talk to God and learn from the Bible. God knows every time you've been mean, grumpy, greedy, selfish, or angry—and He loves you anyway. That deep, lasting, forgiving love is transforming love. That love—God's love—lets you be real when you're with Him, no matter what.

Though the velveteen rabbit had to wait for the boy's love, you don't have to wait for God's transforming love. He loves you like that already. All you have to do is be honest with Him, open your heart to His love, and let Him love you as no one else can, for only God's love can make you real.

Love
Real Love

What Matters Most...

- Understanding that God's love has great power to transform hearts and lives.

- Knowing that God's love is deeper and stronger than human love, looking beyond faults and failings.

- Remembering that you don't have to wait for a special time or place to experience God's love. He loves you right now, just as you are.

- Sensing God's transforming love in your life by allowing yourself to be real when you're with Him.

What Doesn't Matter...

- Whether or not you believe in fairy tales. God's love is no fairy tale. It's real. It's transforming in its power. And it's yours.

- Whether or not your heart is soft toward God or others. God's love can melt a hard heart and make it soft like His.

- Whether or not you've been naughty or nice. While some people may harbor grudges, God loves everyone—no matter what.

- Whether or not you can be real with others. God loves you just as you are. Be yourself. You're loved.

Focus Points...

This is how God showed his love to us: He sent his one and only Son into the world so that we could have life through him.
1 JOHN 4:9 NCV

Nothing above us, nothing below us, nor anything else in the whole world will ever be able to separate us from the love of God.
ROMANS 8:39 NCV

"Though the mountains be shaken and the hills be removed, yet my unfailing love for you will not be shaken nor my covenant of peace be removed," says the LORD.
ISAIAH 54:10 NIV

Keep yourselves in God's love as you wait for the mercy of our Lord Jesus Christ to bring you to eternal life.
JUDE 21 NIV

what really counts

God looks at me—with love. Through the eyes of love, he sees me without blemish, made perfect by the sacrifice of his Son, Jesus. He chose me to be a "jewel in a crown," and fastens me there, not with white glue, but with his promises. God loves me, and he loves you.

ZOE B. METZGER

The meaning of my life is the love of God.

MOTHER TERESA

Love
As I Have Loved You

Since we are all one body in Christ, we belong to each other, and each of us needs all the others.

ROMANS 12:5 NLT

You may have lots of friends or a large family. You may have a cadre of coworkers, too. Yet no matter how many people surround you on a daily basis, you've probably felt lonely at some time, for loneliness is something all people experience. But God has a remedy for loneliness—His love.

From the beginning of creation, God has mended lonely hearts by reaching out to them in creative ways with His love. He provided a helper for Adam so he would not be alone in the garden. He reassured the traveling ancient Israelites that they were not alone, giving them the pillar of cloud and fire as a visible sign of His presence. The psalmist spoke about God's concern for the lonely too, reminding his readers, "God places lonely people in families" (Psalm 68:6 GOD'S WORD). God doesn't want you to feel lonely, either. He wants you to feel accepted, understood, listened to, loved. He opens His arms to you, reassuring you that whenever you feel lonely, you can pray and find comfort, acceptance, and the warmth of His love.

Yet God doesn't stop there. He wants His children to follow His example in their relationships with others by sharing His love with those who feel lonely. Jesus insisted that caring for the lonely was an extension of loving one another. While loving your friends or family is a part of loving others, Jesus condemned those who did not show God's love to people who were hungry, thirsty, alone, sick, or in prison. He reminded His listeners that a refusal to reach out with God's love to such lonely ones was the same as refusing to reach out to Him. To truly "love one another as I have loved you" (John 15:12 NKJV), Jesus urged His listeners to look for ways to love everyone, including the lonely.

There are probably many women in your workplace, church, or neighborhood who struggle with loneliness. Widows and those shut in with chronic illness often feel cut off from others. Single moms, new mothers, and new folks in your community or church may have a hard time finding friends. God wants you to remedy their loneliness with His love. It may take a phone call or a visit, maybe a note or an invitation to coffee. Loneliness happens to everyone, but God's love can heal that hurt. So Jesus says to you, "Speak. Call. Write. Visit. Love—'as I have loved you.'"

Love
As I Have Loved You

What Matters Most...

◉ Learning to love one another as Jesus loves.

◉ Listening and acting on Jesus' admonition to love those who are hungry, thirsty, alone, sick, or in prison, knowing that by doing so, you are truly ministering to Him.

◉ Recognizing that though you may feel lonely, you are never alone or unloved. God promises to always be with you and to love you unceasingly.

◉ Knowing that your visit, words, letter, phone call, or other means of sharing love with someone can help heal the hurt of loneliness.

What Doesn't Matter...

◉ Whether you and someone else share a similar career path, family situation, or circumstance. Loneliness can happen to anyone.

◉ How hurt and alone you have felt in the past or feel right now. God has promised to always be with you. Take comfort; you're never really alone.

◉ How many people you know. Look around you. Someone needs your love—maybe a widow, an orphan, or a stranger.

◉ Whether you're married or single, young or old, career woman or homebody—you can still love others with God's love and ease the loneliness of hurting hearts.

Focus Points...

A new commandment I give to you, that you love one another; as I have loved you, that you also love one another.
JOHN 13:34 NKJV

The alien living with you must be treated as one of your native-born. Love him as yourself.
LEVITICUS 19:34 NIV

Love means doing what God has commanded us, and he has commanded us to love one another, just as you heard from the beginning.
2 JOHN 6 NLT

May the Lord make your love grow more and multiply for each other and for all people so that you will love others as we love you.
1 THESSALONIANS 3:12 NCV

what really counts

Your love for one another will prove to the world that you are my disciples.
JOHN 13:35 NLT

The central purpose of Christ's life ... is to destroy the life of loneliness and to establish here on earth the life of love.

THOMAS WOLFE

Whatever in love's name is truly done to free the bound and lift the fallen one, is done to Christ.

JOHN GREENLEAF WHITTIER

What Matters Most to Me About
Love

God's unconditional love can set you free, can let you be you, and can give you eyes to see others as He sees them. Reflect on His love as you journal your answers below.

◉ *Prayerfully write down your own definition of love. How can you apply this definition to those in your family, your neighborhood, your church? Record some specific ways here. Return to this page in a few months to check your progress.*

_____

_____

_____

_____

_____

_____

_____

◉ *List some characteristics of God's love. Compare these traits with the way you show love to God or others. What do you need to change in your life so that your love and its expression are more like God's love?*

_____

_____

_____

_____

_____

_____

_____

◎ *Think back on a time when you felt loved and accepted. What were some of the things that others said or did to make you feel that way? How can you show lonely people in your church or community these same hallmarks of love and acceptance?*

_____

_____

_____

_____

_____

_____

_____

_____

◎ *Journal your thoughts on God's unconditional love and the ways that such love can transform you and make you more real with Him. How can God's unconditional love make you more real with others, too?*

_____

_____

_____

_____

_____

_____

_____

_____

_____

Love does not delight in evil but rejoices with the truth. It always protects, always trusts, always hopes, always perseveres. Love never fails.

1 CORINTHIANS 13:6–8 NIV

HEAVEN

An Introduction

> Rejoice because your names are written in heaven.
> LUKE 10:20 NKJV

what really counts

Heaven might come up occasionally in your conversations with others. Someone might comment that a tasty morsel or beautiful gown was "heavenly." John Denver likened West Virginia to the countryside of heaven. But the kingdom of heaven is so much more than you can possibly imagine. The book of Revelation describes the city of heaven in terms of harps, crowns, choirs, and angels to suggest the splendor, joy, and timelessness of eternity in God's kingdom.

Yet Jesus indicated that the kingdom of heaven was more than just a place to look forward to for the future. Jesus said that God's kingdom was present right now, that God's kingdom was among people in the hearts of those who loved Him. He said that you didn't have to wait to die to experience a bit of heaven. Jesus said heaven is a spiritual destination that a transformed heart can experience right now.

That little bit of heaven in your heart can have an unusual effect on you. It can actually make you feel a bit homesick for God's hometown—heaven. But that heart-tug to head home to heaven is a good thing because it fills you with hope that someday you will reach your eternal home.

So when the talk of something "heavenly" comes up in conversation, let it remind you that heaven is a place for your heart right now, a place for you some-day in the future, too, and the place where God waits to see you face-to-face.

> There is a heaven, for ever, day by day, the upward longing of my soul doth tell me so.
>
> PAUL LAURENCE DUNBAR

Heaven
The Kingdom of Heaven

> It has been given to you to know the
> mysteries of the kingdom of heaven.
> MATTHEW 13:11 NKJV

Visit an Internet map site and you'll find that you can travel from Hell to Paradise in twenty-four different ways. That's because twenty-four towns in the United States claim the name of "Paradise," while only one town in Michigan boasts the name "Hell." Yet no matter how hard you search road maps or map sites, you won't find "Heaven" anywhere— no matter what folks in West Virginia claim. Mapmakers and town-namers instinctively know heaven is not a place you can reach with trains, planes, or automobiles. Heaven is a spiritual destination, for the kingdom of heaven is the kingdom of God.

The book of Revelation is a gold mine of images about heaven. John wrote about a city with gates of pearl, walls of jewels, and streets of gold, shining "with the glory of God" (Revelation 21:11 NIV). A river runs through this heavenly city, and on each side of the river stands the tree of life, bearing continuous fruit. The sound of music fills the air as people and angels join voices together praising God. Darkness, death, sadness, and pain have no place here. They've been replaced by God's glorious light, life, joy, and presence. The Bible proclaims that heaven truly is a wonderful place, a kingdom where God's will is always enacted and where believers will live joyfully for all eternity.

Yet there is a mystery, too, to heaven—a mysterious state of the heart. John the Baptist urged listeners to change their hearts and lives because the kingdom of heaven was near. Jesus picked up where John left off, announcing that the kingdom of heaven wasn't just some faraway place for people to gather after this life is over. Jesus said He was bringing God's kingdom to earth right now. In a supernatural way, when God forgives your faults and failings, cleanses your heart, and claims you as His child, an eternal change takes place in your spirit. Though you won't take up permanent residence in God's Holy City of heaven until you die, through Jesus Christ you are already a citizen of the kingdom of heaven. And through Christ, you already have a bit of heaven in your heart.

People often think heaven is somewhere "up" in the stratosphere. But heaven isn't "up" or anywhere else you can humanly reach. Heaven is a spiritual destination to be found in an eternal Holy City and in your forgiven heart.

Heaven
The Kingdom of Heaven

What Matters Most...

◎ Realizing that heaven is not humanly reachable. You can't travel to it or earn it. Entrance to heaven comes through God alone.

◎ Realizing that heaven is the kingdom of God, the place where God reigns supreme.

◎ Realizing that heaven is the spiritual, joyful destination for forgiven souls.

◎ Realizing that heaven is already present in your forgiven heart. Praise God today for this wonderful transformation and gift.

What Doesn't Matter...

◎ How well you read maps. Since you can't get to heaven by conventional means, no maps are required.

◎ How well you can sense heaven in your heart. Spend some time with God in prayer to rekindle the sense of heaven.

◎ How well you sing. When you get to heaven, your voice will be perfect so that you can joyously praise God.

◎ How well you live. You can't do anything to earn heaven. Only God's forgiveness can bring heaven to you and your heart.

Focus Points...

The kingdom of God is present not in talk but in power.
1 CORINTHIANS 4:20 NCV

The right time has come. The kingdom of God is near. Change your hearts and lives and believe the Good News!
MARK 1:15 NCV

Not all those who say that I am their Lord will enter the kingdom of heaven. The only people who will enter the kingdom of heaven are those who do what my Father in heaven wants.
MATTHEW 7:21 NCV

Do not fear, little flock, for it is your Father's good pleasure to give you the kingdom.
LUKE 12:32 NKJV

what really counts

Just as my Father has given me a kingdom, I also give you a kingdom so you may eat and drink at my table in my kingdom.
LUKE 22:29–30 NCV

Theological beliefs may get one into a church, but not into the kingdom of heaven.
STANLEY I. STUBER

When the eyes of the soul looking out meet the eyes of God looking in, heaven has begun right here on earth.
A. W. TOZER

Heaven
Homeward Bound

> They were looking for a better place, a heavenly homeland.
>
> HEBREWS 11:16 NLT

Whether you've moved a dozen times or enjoyed permanent residency in one place for many years, there's something comforting in the three little words "I'm going home." It may be a cramped apartment, a starter home, or open land where the deer and antelope play, but wherever you hang your heart, that's home. It's familiar. It's a respite from the world. It's the place where you belong. Home.

Hadad knew that comforting sense of home. As a young boy, he had run away to Egypt and had enjoyed great success, marrying into the king's family. His son was raised in the royal palace with the king's own children. But one day Hadad felt the deep heart-tug of homesickness. Though he had everything money could buy, though he had all the power a person could want, Hadad just had to get home. Nothing else would do. The longing for home was too strong, and he was homeward bound without delay.

Have you ever felt that way? Maybe you felt the ache of homesickness when you were a child at summer camp. Maybe you've been away on vacation or an extended business trip and just couldn't wait to open your own front door again. That longing for home is something God has built into your heart. But God wants that longing for home to extend beyond your front door. The Bible reminds you that you are already a citizen of God's kingdom of heaven, and God actually wants you to long for heaven, to be homesick for your heavenly home. The apostle Paul indicated that God "puts a little of heaven in our hearts so that we'll never settle for less" (2 Corinthians 5:5 MSG). With eternity beating in your heart, being homesick for heaven is a good thing.

Jesus told His disciples He would prepare a place in heaven for all those who put their trust in Him. Because you are God's child, that's a promise you can rely on. Jesus is readying a home for you in heaven—a place that's comforting, that's familiar. A home where you belong, where you fit, where you are always loved. This world is not your real home. Your mailing address won't be your eternal residence. It's okay to feel a longing for a better place, for a perfect home, especially if that home is in heaven, because heaven is really the place where you and your heart belong.

Heaven
Homeward Bound

What Matters Most...

◎ Recognizing that you have a permanent, eternal place of residency in God's hometown.

◎ Knowing that you carry a little bit of eternity in your heart that will nudge you toward your heavenly home.

◎ Looking forward to a change of address. God already has a home ready for you.

◎ Relying on the promise that Jesus is readying your eternal, heavenly home, where you will live in peace with God forever.

What Doesn't Matter...

◎ Where you live right now. Your earthly home won't be your eternal home. God has promised you a home with Him in heaven.

◎ How many times you've moved. In heaven, God has a perfect place ready for you. No more moving needed.

◎ Whether or not your current home is comfortable, quiet, or stress-free. Your heavenly home will be perfect, made just for you.

◎ How much you know about heaven. Read the Bible to familiarize yourself with your heart's eternal home.

Focus Points...

I go to prepare a place for you. And if I go and prepare a place for you, I will come again and receive you to Myself; that where I am, there you may be also.
JOHN 14:2–3 NKJV

Our homeland is in heaven, and we are waiting for our Savior, the Lord Jesus Christ.
PHILIPPIANS 3:20 NCV

He who has prepared us for this very thing is God, who also has given us the Spirit as a guarantee.
2 CORINTHIANS 5:5 NKJV

We know that our body—the tent we live in here on earth—will be destroyed. But when that happens, God will have a house for us ... a home in heaven that will last forever.
2 CORINTHIANS 5:1 NCV

what
really
counts

Though we live on earth, we have already established legal residence in heaven.

ERWIN W. LUTZER

Faith's journey ends in welcome to the weary, and heaven, our heart's true home, will come at last.

FREDERICK W. FABER

What Matters Most to Me About
Heaven

Heaven is a glorious destination for believers. Since you never know when you'll find yourself on your way to heaven, why not spend some time thinking about your eternal home?

◉ *You will be able to rest from your work in heaven, but you won't have to rest from your delights. What things make you happy? What things would you be delighted to find or do in God's kingdom of heaven? Start to make your list here.*

_____

_____

_____

_____

_____

_____

◉ *Sit quietly and consider what Jesus said about the kingdom of heaven being with you right now. How does that make you feel? What can you do to share this feeling or sense of heaven with someone else?*

_____

_____

_____

_____

_____

_____

Remember a time when you might have been homesick as a child. Record here what that felt like. Now consider how feeling homesick for heaven could be similar and yet different. What are the bad things about feeling homesick? What are the good things about feeling homesick for heaven?

_____

_____

_____

_____

_____

_____

_____

_____

_____

As you contemplate being homeward bound for heaven, compose a prayer to God, confessing your failings, requesting His forgiveness, and asking Him to make you the person He wants you to be. Then thank Him for preparing an eternal home for you with Him.

_____

_____

_____

_____

_____

_____

_____

_____

_____

HEAVEN

Come, you blessed of My Father, inherit the kingdom prepared for you from the foundation of the world.
MATTHEW 25:34 NKJV

GOD'S WORD

An Introduction

> Your word, O LORD, is eternal; it stands firm in the heavens.
>
> PSALM 119:89 NIV

what really counts

Though written language has been a part of civilized society for millennia, God's Word, the Bible, has been available for people to read only a few hundred years. In 1382, John Wycliffe, a religious reformer, translated the Bible into English. Wycliffe knew how hard it was to embrace something that was difficult to understand. By translating the Bible into English, Wycliffe hoped common people would finally be able to read and understand the Bible in their native tongue.

The psalmist knew how beneficial it was to love and understand the Bible. The longest chapter in Scripture is Psalm 119—a psalm dedicated to learning, loving, and understanding the Bible more and more. That's what God wants for you. He wants you to learn to love His Word and receive the blessings reserved for those who do so.

John Wycliffe understood that the Bible is to be a light in believers' lives, a guide for their decisions, and a means to help people grow closer to God, too. He wanted believers in medieval England to use the Bible to measure their faith. It's the same for you today. Though learning to love the Bible is a start in the right direction, to truly grow in your faith and relationship with God, you need to use the Bible as your guidebook for living, your sourcebook for decision making. Learning to love the Bible *and* using the Bible to help you grow closer to God will bring abundant blessings to your life and will please Him.

> The Bible is a page torn out of the great volume of human life; torn by the hand of God and annotated by his Spirit.
>
> JOSEPH PARKER

God's Word
Gotta Love It

> I love your written instructions.
> PSALM 119:119 GOD'S WORD

Two girlfriends hug bowls of popcorn while watching a favorite rental from the video store. They've seen the movie so often they can repeat the dialogue with the characters. The ending never changes, yet both sigh audibly when the final credits roll. Inevitably one friend will turn to the other and ask, "Want to watch it again?"

There's something about the things you love that make you want to keep them close, to experience them again, to renew the comfort and security they bring, or in some way hang on to the love they make you feel so deeply. But did you know that God wants you to have that kind of love for the Bible, too? The longest chapter in Scripture is tucked into its very middle in the book of Psalms, chapter 119. And what's the subject of this chapter? The Bible and how to love it more and more.

If asked, you might confess to a love of many things: chocolate, swing music, Christmas, puppies, old movies, etc. But how did you come to love these things? After your first taste of them? Probably not. Your love for something usually grows with each successive experience. In the same way, your appreciation for the Bible can grow with each reading. As you experience and learn from the Bible, you become more familiar with it and find it becomes a comfort to your life. As you keep on reading and learning, that familiarity grows exponentially into a deep love for Scripture. It's a natural progression to a spiritual process.

God also has set aside special blessings for you when you value, care for, and love the Bible. Treasuring the Bible will fill your heart with His everlasting peace. You'll have insights about life that others might miss. Loving the Bible will revive your weary spirit, bring you joy, and "give you a long and satisfying life" (Proverbs 3:2 NLT). Because its pages reveal everything there is to know about God, your love for the Bible will also help you see and understand God and His ways. And when you love the Bible, God promises to give you wisdom and understanding, guidance and grace, light in the darkness, and His love in return. So read the Bible. Search its pages. Come to love it and delight in it. In this way, the Bible will become light and life to you.

God's Word
Gotta Love It

What Matters Most...

- Knowing that God wants you to have a deep-down love in your heart for the Bible.

- Knowing that as you become more familiar with the Bible, it will become a comfort to your life and a light to your path.

- Knowing that your love for the Bible will help you see and understand God and His ways.

- Knowing that God promises to give you wisdom, guidance, joy, and refreshment when you love and delight in reading, searching, and understanding the Bible.

What **Doesn't** Matter...

- That it seems strange to love a book. The strangeness of anything fades the more you do it. Learn to love the Bible by reading it often.

- That you usually skip Psalm 119 because the chapter is so-o-o long. Be adventuresome. Read the whole chapter.

- That you don't always understand the Bible. You're in good company.

- That you're not sure how to love the Bible. It's simple. Read the Bible consistently, noting what God uses to touch your heart each time.

Focus Points...

I inherited your book on living; it's mine forever—what a gift! And how happy it makes me!
PSALM 119:111 MSG

Oh, how I love your teachings! They are in my thoughts all day long.
PSALM 119:97 GOD'S WORD

I remember your ancient laws, O LORD, and I find comfort in them ... Your decrees are the theme of my song wherever I lodge.
PSALM 119:52, 54 NIV

I love Your commandments more than gold, yes, than fine gold! Therefore all Your precepts concerning all things I consider to be right.
PSALM 119:127–128 NKJV

what really counts

Those who love your teachings will find true peace, and nothing will defeat them.
PSALM 119:165 NCV

When you have read the Bible, you will know it is the word of God because you have found it the key to your own heart, your own happiness, and your own duty.
WOODROW WILSON

The highest earthly enjoyments are but a shadow of the joy I find in reading God's Word.
LADY JANE GREY

117

God's Word
Gotta Use It

Your word is a lamp to my feet
and a light to my path.
PSALM 119:105 NKJV

Internet map sites are a great help to women who have to travel between unfamiliar locations. With a few keystrokes, you can request explicit driving directions between your points of departure and arrival. You can also print a map with your route highlighted so that you won't get lost. However, one lady arrived very late for a wedding despite accessing an Internet map site. She typed everything correctly and printed out pages of directions and maps. The only problem—she never referenced them as she drove down the road. Maps—even the best of them—aren't much help unless you use them.

The apostle Paul recognized the needfulness for a spiritual road map for his young protégé, Timothy. Timothy had been raised in a home with a godly mother and grandmother. He had been taught the Scriptures as a young boy. As a young man trying to fill Paul's shoes as the new pastor of the church in Ephesus, Timothy was feeling overwhelmed. He didn't know what to do about church friction and false teachers. He thought he was too young to influence older believers or give guidance to widows and orphans.

Paul lovingly advised Timothy to "remain faithful to the things you have been taught" (2 Timothy 3:14 NLT). He urged him to use the Bible as his life map. Paul assured the young man that the Bible would make him wise and also provide a sure guide for him as he led others in their faith. The Bible would be Timothy's road map to highlight the right path and emphasize what needed to be corrected. He reminded Timothy that whatever duty he had to do, whatever service he was called upon to perform, the Bible could show him everything he should do to accomplish those things—and do them well.

The Bible can be a spiritual road map for your faith journey, too. But it won't do you any good if you leave it on the coffee table and never read it. Open the Bible. Read it often. Become familiar with it. Study His road map to life—on your own or with a group from your church or neighborhood. The Bible can answer all your questions about what to believe, how to act, what to choose, and how to live. Don't get lost on your spiritual journey. Make good use of the road map of the Bible to make sure you're headed in the right direction.

God's Word
Gotta Use It

What Matters Most...

◎ Recognizing that the Bible is your spiritual guide to living the life God wants you to live.

◎ Remaining faithful to the things you have learned from the Bible.

◎ Remembering that the Bible will be a help to you if you read it, learn from it, and apply those lessons to your daily life.

◎ Finding time regularly to explore the Bible to find out how to live, what to believe, and what decisions to make.

What Doesn't Matter...

◎ How often you've made wrong turns while traveling. The Bible can keep you from making wrong turns in your faith journey.

◎ Whether or not you learned about the Bible when you were younger. When it comes to the Bible, you're never too old to start learning.

◎ How old your copy of the Bible is. The Bible is still current and useful.

◎ Whether or not you've used the Bible as a life map. Start down the road to a closer relationship with Him.

Focus Points...

Every part of Scripture is God-breathed and useful one way or another—showing us truth, exposing our rebellion, correcting our mistakes, training us to live God's way.
2 TIMOTHY 3:16 MSG

The word of God is full of living power. It is sharper than the sharpest knife, cutting deep into our innermost thoughts and desires. It exposes us for what we really are.
HEBREWS 4:12 NLT

These commands are like a lamp; this teaching is like a light. And the correction that comes from them will help you have life.
PROVERBS 6:23 NCV

God wants the combination of his steady, constant calling and warm, personal counsel in Scripture to come to characterize us, keeping us alert for whatever he will do next.
ROMANS 15:4 MSG

what really counts

The Bible is God's chart for you to steer by, to keep you from the bottom of the sea, and to show you where the harbor is, and how to reach it without running on rocks or bars.
HENRY WARD BEECHER

To what greater inspiration and counsel can we turn than to the imperishable truth to be found in this treasure house, the Bible?
QUEEN ELIZABETH II

What Matters Most to Me About
God's Word

God speaks to you in your day-to-day experiences through the pages of the Bible. You only need to take the time to read and listen to what He tells you. Start by thinking about these things.

◉ *To truly begin to love anything, you have to experience it on a regular basis. Write a prayer committing yourself to a regular time of reading and studying the Bible. Follow through on that prayer by making sure you have a copy of the Bible available in a translation you can easily read.*

_____

_____

_____

what
really
counts

_____

_____

◉ *Open the Bible to Psalm 119. Pray as you read two or three of its sections. Ask God to make the Bible come alive to you. Then list here some of the benefits the psalmist said come from reading, understanding, and loving the Bible.*

_____

_____

_____

_____

_____

_____

⊙ *The Bible is the source of His written communication with you. Record here a verse from the meditations above that divulged something about God or the Bible that you didn't know before. How does that information change your view about God, the Bible, or your life?*

_____

_____

_____

_____

_____

_____

_____

_____

⊙ *Paul wanted Timothy to use the Bible as his guidebook for living. Look up Romans 12 or Philippians 2 in the Bible, exploring ways that these verses could help guide you in your spiritual growth. What suggestions from these passages could you apply to your life right now?*

_____

_____

_____

_____

_____

_____

_____

_____

The grass withers, the flower fades, but
the word of our God stands forever.
ISAIAH 40:8 NKJV

THE FUTURE

An Introduction

> Do not boast about tomorrow, for you do not know what a day may bring forth.
>
> PROVERBS 27:1 NKJV

what really counts

Schoolchildren busily fold paper into quarters and eighths, tucking corners into triangles until their handiwork resembles a multimouthed puppet. By opening and closing the leaves of this origami fortune-teller, inquisitive minds can ask questions of the future, like "What color hair will my boyfriend have?" or "When I grow up, will I be a doctor, lawyer, or ballet dancer?"

Youngsters aren't the only ones who want to know what the future will bring. All people have an itch to know what will happen before it happens. Knowing what to expect makes life less scary. However, only God truly knows what the future holds. In fact, to face the future without feeling afraid or vulnerable, the Bible advises you to keep your focus on Him. God is in control of your future, so you can face anything that happens with the assurance that He has everything in control.

Sometimes it's hard to face the future because you're still stuck in the past. Past hurts, past disappointments, or past failures can keep your heart churned up and limit your forward progress. The Bible reminds you to give up that backward look, to put past things behind you, and to look forward to what God has in store for you.

You don't need a folded-paper soothsayer to point you down the right road to the future. Just follow God's guidelines: forget the past; focus on Him; face the future. And remember, no matter what the future holds, God is in control.

> We should all be concerned about the future; because we will have to spend the rest of our lives there.
>
> CHARLES KETTERING

The Future
Face the Future

> Do not look behind you . . . lest you be destroyed.
>
> GENESIS 19:17 NKJV

You've probably heard the Bible story about Sodom and Gomorrah. In this action-packed tale from the Bible, Abraham finds out that Sodom and Gomorrah are going to be destroyed. Lot, Abraham's nephew, lives in Sodom, so Abraham asks God for help. God sends some angels to rescue Lot and his family before the cities are destroyed. As Lot and his family escape the burning fireballs of brimstone, Lot's wife looks back, and *wham!* She's turned into a pillar of salt. Wow, what a story!

Lot's wife ended her days on earth in such a spectacular way because she disobeyed the direct command of God's angel, who told the family not to look back, "lest you be destroyed" (Genesis 19:17 NKJV). Looking back became a dangerous thing for Lot's family to do. Likewise, looking back can have a paralyzing influence on you, too. Failure to let go of the past and relinquish prior hurts, losses, or mistakes can keep you from growing free and strong in your emotional and spiritual lives. Looking back and harboring hatred, condemnation, or prejudice can immobilize you and keep you from future blessings. Always looking back can turn your spirit into a rock-hard pillar of salt, but getting beyond the past can open your heart to the future.

The apostle Paul was a living example of this principle. In the early chapters of Acts, you find Paul persecuting Christians and even killing a few at every turn. Yet while traveling the Damascus road, Paul met Jesus in a vision, and his life was instantly changed. He then could write a letter to the Philippians and say with conviction, "Because God has forgiven me and no longer remembers my mistakes, I'm forgetting about those things, too. I'm going to keep my eyes on the future and follow Christ."

Keeping photos or mementos of memories can be good, but focusing on the past won't bring you into the future God has in store for you. You may have to let those mementos go if they keep you tied to past dreams that can't be fulfilled or debts that can't be repaid. To enjoy the days to come, you may have to change some habits or confront fears that have dogged you for a lifetime. Let go of prior things that keep you from growing in the fullness of God. To openly face the future, forget the past.

The Future
Face the Future

What Matters Most...

◎ Understanding that memories and mementos can be good things, but living a life that constantly looks back with regret, fear, or longing will only keep you from blessings in the future.

◎ Recognizing that a failure to let go of past hurts, losses, or mistakes is not spiritually or emotionally healthy. Only by putting the past behind can you truly look forward to the future.

◎ Believing that God can do for you what He did for Paul —grant you the grace to pursue a future of following Christ. God will do it; just ask.

What **Doesn't** Matter...

◎ What mistakes you've made in the past. God promises to forgive and forget your mistakes.

◎ What other people have done or said to you. Past hurts can hurt, but constantly reliving them keeps you spiritually stuck.

◎ How tough it can be to forget your past. Pray, trust, and follow God's guidance.

◎ How hard your heart has become. God's touch can melt any heart.

Focus Points...

Lot's wife looked back as she was following along behind him, and she became a pillar of salt.
GENESIS 19:26 NLT

Do not call to mind the former things, or ponder things of the past.
ISAIAH 43:18 NASB

Look, I will make new heavens and a new earth, and people will not remember the past or think about those things.
ISAIAH 65:17 NCV

Jesus said to him, "No one, after putting his hand to the plow and looking back, is fit for the kingdom of God."
LUKE 9:62 NASB

what really counts

He who has commanded us not to look back when we have put our hands to the plough does as he would have us do—he does not regard the past sins of a soul which seeks his kingdom.

SAINT CYRAN

By trusting in Jesus, we discover the only One who can release us from the guilt of the past, the only One who can relieve us from fear of the future, and the only One who can free us to live today, today.

JACOB D. EPPINGA

The Future
Never Helpless

Since no man knows the future,
who can tell him what is to come?
ECCLESIASTES 8:7 NIV

What do these situations have in common: the start of a new job, the week you wait between a medical test and its result, and a blind date with your best friend's boyfriend's best friend? The answer? Future uncertainty—and lots of it. A new job could ask more of you than you're able to give. A test result could mean a different life span. And that blind date? It could be either fun or a fiasco. The future is so full of unknowns you can often feel helpless, vulnerable, and scared.

Hezekiah faced a future that was so frightening the Bible records the story three times—in 2 Kings 18; 2 Chronicles 32; and Isaiah 36. According to biblical scholars, when the Bible says something once, it's a good thing to remember it. Repeating the story or statement a second time adds emphasis to it, as when a teacher says to a student, "Pay attention, please." But when the Bible repeats something three times, God really wants you to listen up, to take this story to heart,

130

because hidden within it are major, life-transforming lessons. So what's hidden within Hezekiah's story? The key to the future.

Hezekiah's people were facing sure destruction from Sennacherib's army. One of Sennacherib's generals came to Hezekiah's palace bearing a note with terms for the king's surrender. The note insulted God's character and maligned His power. Sennacherib's soldiers taunted the Israelites, too, with vicious descriptions of what they would do to the people if they didn't force their king to surrender. The future looked bleak. Yet King Hezekiah's first response to this frightening situation wasn't fear, verbal combat, or a sense of helplessness. Hezekiah didn't know what the future held for him or his people, but he did know who was in charge of the future—God. So Hezekiah prayed and asked God what to do.

When you face the unknowns of the future, you have a choice. You can worry and fret and fall to pieces, feeling helpless, hopeless, and vulnerable. Or you can choose to follow Hezekiah's example, unsure, maybe, of what the future holds, but very sure about God and His power to make your future into what He wants it to be. Never feel helpless about the future again. Take your scary future and unknowns to God in prayer. Ask Him to show you what to do, and trust Him to make your future a good one.

The Future
Never Helpless

What Matters Most...

◉ Being aware that God always knows your unknowns. Trust Him to work things out for your good.

◉ Knowing that when the future looks bleak, there is no need to fear. God is in control of the future.

◉ Believing that God has everything in control and has the power to make your future what He wants it to be.

◉ Relinquishing your fear of future unknowns, submitting those scary things to God in prayer, and trusting Him to work everything out for your good.

What Doesn't Matter...

◉ How many unknowns you'll face this week, this month, this year. All your unknowns are in God's hands. He knows the future. Trust Him.

◉ How frightening the future can seem. Just remember who is in charge of the future—God. He will take care of you.

◉ How well you respond to scary situations. Pray first, and be assured that God is in control.

◉ How many keys you carry. You'll always have room for another key, especially this spiritual one: no matter what the future holds, God holds the future.

Focus Points...

"Stop crying; don't let your eyes fill with tears. You will be rewarded for your work!" says the LORD ..."So there is hope for you in the future."
JEREMIAH 31:16–17 NCV

There is surely a future hope for you, and your hope will not be cut off.
PROVERBS 23:18 NIV

I know the thoughts that I think toward you, says the LORD, thoughts of peace and not of evil, to give you a future and a hope.
JEREMIAH 29:11 NKJV

She is strong and is respected by the people. She looks forward to the future with joy.
PROVERBS 31:25 NCV

We do not know what the future holds, but we know the One who holds the future, the One in whose pierced hands reposes all power in heaven and on earth.

WALTER B. KNIGHT

The unknown puts adventure into life. It gives us something to sharpen our souls on. The unexpected around the corner gives a sense of anticipation and surprise. Thank God for the unknown future.

E. STANLEY JONES

133

What Matters Most to Me About
The Future

As you work on forgetting the past and focusing on your future without fear, consider these questions and remember: God's promises about the future are certain because everything is under His control.

◎ *Think about a time when holding on to your past prevented you from moving forward. Record that experience here. What eventually happened and what did you learn in that situation? How can that lesson help you trust God for your future?*

_____

_____

_____

_____

_____

_____

_____

_____

◎ *Though holding on to the past can be limiting, God instructed the Israelites to build a memorial to remember His past provision in the future. Record some ways that you can turn your personal mementos into memorials that will turn your heart toward God and help you face the future.*

_____

_____

_____

_____

_____

_____

○ Some people seek unusual means to discover what will happen in the future. Yet only God truly knows what the future holds. Believing this, what should your attitude be toward the future? How can having a strong faith in God help you face future unknowns?

_____

_____

_____

_____

_____

_____

_____

_____

○ Though the future is unknown to human beings, God knows everything about the future. He also promises future blessings for His children. How can this knowledge give you hope for the coming days and months and relieve your anxieties about the future?

_____

_____

_____

_____

_____

_____

_____

_____

The end of the world is coming soon. Therefore, be earnest and disciplined in your prayers.

1 PETER 4:7 NLT

WORSHIP

An Introduction

> Come, let us worship and bow down; let us kneel before the LORD our Maker.
>
> PSALM 95:6 NKJV

what really counts

When God gave the ancient Israelites the instructions for building the tent they would use for worship, He also set aside an Israelite family—the Levites—to take care of all the duties of this worship center, including the music program. Because music was so important to the worship of God, those Levites who were musicians were exempt from other duties. They would compose, sing, and play songs of praise and worship around the clock. Yet the Levites weren't the only performers of these songs. According to God's plan, all the Israelites were to participate and sing the songs of praise and worship that the Levites penned.

Though the worship of God has changed in style, format, and place since the days of the ancient Levites, music still plays an important part in showing reverence and love for God. Whether or not you have the voice of an angel, praising God—whether at home alone or with others in your church—by lifting your voice in song is still one of the best ways you can enter into close communion, fellowship, and the worship of God.

However, when the music and singing stop, your worship shouldn't end. Everything you do, everything you say, everywhere you go, every thought you think, and every aspect of your life should be lived as an act of worship. You don't have to wait for a special day of the week to worship God. Worship Him daily—with your voice *and* with your life.

Worship—the only gift we can bring to God that he himself has not first given to us.
ISOBEL RALSTON

Worship
Sing to the Lord

Sing to him, sing praise to him;
tell of all his wonderful acts.

1 Chronicles 16:9 NIV

what really counts

Have you ever seen a children's program where little ones have to sing a song? The preschool singers are usually the best. Maybe not musically, but what they lack in musicality they make up for in volume. Heads held high. Mouths wide open. Lungs filled to bursting. Vocal cords belting out the song with total abandon. The perfection of the children's performance doesn't matter, for the parents in the audience will point with pride to both their on- and off-key offspring.

But how about you? Do you have a marvelous singing voice, or are you one of those alone-in-the-car rock stars? A songbird that belts it out only when the noise of traffic drowns out your off-key musicality? Whatever your vocal abilities, don't fret. God doesn't care what you sound like. He just wants you to use your voice in worship. God loves to hear you sing, just as families love to hear their pint-sized virtuosos. Perfect pitch isn't required to worship God.

Singing in worship—the musical voicing of praise to God—has been a practice of His children since the time of the ancient Israelites. Whenever a major event occurred in the life of Israel—the ark of the covenant returning to Jerusalem, the dedication of the temple, the army marching into battle, the coronation of a king, the celebration of Passover—the people of Israel would join their voices in song, praising God for His majesty and worshiping Him for His powerful acts on their behalf. Ordinary worship in the tabernacle or temple included singing, too, by ordinary folks with ordinary voices, praising God with their often off-key rejoicing. The concern wasn't about their performance, but rather it was about their intent to worship, praise, and adore God through song.

The apostle Paul urged God's children to sing psalms, hymns, and spiritual songs together as a way to connect with God. Yet you don't have to wait for a specific weekend worship time to sing to God. Use the moments in the shower to croon "Good Morning!" to your heavenly Father. Take traffic delays in stride by belting out a favorite hymn or Scripture chorus. Sing while doing your chores, while walking the dog, while getting ready for bed. No matter how talented a vocalist you are (or aren't), God longs to hear your voice lifted in worship to Him. So "sing and make music in your heart to the Lord" (Ephesians 5:19 NIV).

Worship
Sing to the Lord

What Matters Most...

◎ Knowing that God's children have worshiped in song whenever major events occurred. You also can use the high points in your life as times for worship and praise songs.

◎ Remembering that your performance ability isn't what counts when it comes to worshiping God in song. Your heart's intent is what's important.

◎ Using your voice to worship God—any time, any place, for any reason.

What Doesn't Matter...

◎ Your age. Preschoolers can worship God with simple songs; the aged, too, can sing, even if voices crack and warble. Whatever your age, lift your voice and sing.

◎ Your vocal range. One or two notes up and down the musical scale form some of the most beautiful worship chants in church history. Use whatever vocal range you have and sing.

◎ Your musical training. Ordinary people without musical training have been worshiping God.

◎ Your shyness. When you worship God, you're not in a contest to see who can sing the best.

Focus Points...

Shout to the LORD, all the earth; break out in praise and sing for joy! Sing your praise to the LORD with the harp, with the harp and melodious song.
PSALM 98:4–5 NLT

Oh, sing to the LORD a new song! Sing to the LORD, all the earth. Sing to the LORD, bless His name; proclaim the good news of His salvation.
PSALM 96:1 2 NKJV

I will sing to the LORD as long as I live; I will sing praise to my God while I have my being.
PSALM 104:33 NKJV

Sing praises to God, sing praises; sing praises to our King, sing praises. For God is the King of all the earth; sing praises with a skillful psalm.
PSALM 47:6–7 NASB

what really counts

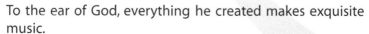

To the ear of God, everything he created makes exquisite music.

OSWALD CHAMBERS

Worship is not haphazard music done poorly, not even great music done merely as a performance; we celebrate God when we enjoy and participate in music to His glory.

RONALD ALLEN

Worship
A Living Sacrifice

Offer your bodies as living sacrifices, holy and pleasing to God—this is your spiritual act of worship.

ROMANS 12:1 NIV

what really counts

Mention the word *worship,* and some folks envision an informal style of singing. Others connect worship with a time when they gather to listen to a pastor's discourse. Yet there is more to worship than songs and sermons. According to Scripture, worship is to be the celebration, praise, adoration, and reverence by which God receives honor. Worship should include trust, joy, awe, and confession of wrongdoing, thanksgiving, music, song, and the reading of the Bible. However, worship shouldn't be limited to what you do or say in church once or twice a week. The apostle Paul contended the true worship of God revolves around a lifestyle choice, a conscious decision to give yourself willingly and wholeheartedly as a living sacrifice to God.

Nice idea, right? But how does someone become a living sacrifice? How do you live a lifestyle of worship? Though it sounds difficult, you probably already do some of it without realizing it. For example, if you've ever left a warm bed in the middle of the night to help a sick friend, made a call and cheered a lonely neighbor, or sent a card to console a grieving widow, you've already sacrificed your time for others. To live a lifestyle of worship, to become a living sacrifice for God, all you need to do is more of what you're already doing.

It works like this: A lifestyle of worship seeks to treat others as Christ would treat them—looking beyond people to their needs and helping wherever possible; sharing time, talents, words, and wisdom with others to help them grow stronger in their faith; providing a safe place of refuge for those with hurting hearts and pointing them to God as their true source of refuge. A lifestyle of worship seeks to love God completely and entirely by spending time each day in prayer and communication with Him, earnestly studying the Bible to learn more about Him and how He wants you to live, and constantly praising Him for His goodness, mercy, and grace to you. To become a living sacrifice for God, you'll also strive to fulfill the purpose God has given you, do the tasks He sends your way, and be His light wherever He sends you.

So expand your view of worship. Take Paul's admonition to heart. Choose to be a living sacrifice, and thereby make your life "your spiritual act of worship" (Romans 12:1 NIV).

Worship
A Living Sacrifice

What Matters Most...

◎ Realizing that the worship of God includes many different elements: trust, joy, awe, confession, thanksgiving, music, song, and the reading of the Bible.

◎ Understanding that the worship of God shouldn't be limited to what you do in church once or twice a week.

◎ Remembering that the true worship of God includes a lifestyle choice, a conscious decision to give yourself willingly and wholeheartedly as a living sacrifice to God.

◎ Making your whole life an act of worship by striving to fulfill God's purposes wherever He sends you.

What Doesn't Matter...

◎ How often you go to church. Worship involves more than church attendance. Worship encompasses an attitude of the heart that seeks to honor God in everything.

◎ What style of church music you prefer. Though music is an element of worship, true worship embodies more than song styles. Expand your worship viewpoint.

◎ That you don't think you can live a life of worship. Admit your fears to God, and pray for His strength.

◎ That you feel you're not talented enough. Well, guess what? No special talents are required to live a life that honors God. Just do what you do, but do it for Him.

Focus Points...

You are to live clean, innocent lives as children of God in a dark world full of crooked and perverse people. Let your lives shine brightly before them.
PHILIPPIANS 2:15 NLT

It's the praising life that honors me. As soon as you set your foot on the Way, I'll show you my salvation.
PSALM 50:23 MSG

God is building you, as living stones, into his spiritual temple. What's more, you are God's holy priests, who offer the spiritual sacrifices that please him because of Jesus Christ.
1 PETER 2:5 NLT

Let us always offer to God our sacrifice of praise, coming from lips that speak his name. Do not forget to do good to others, and share with them, because such sacrifices please God.
HEBREWS 13:15–16 NCV

what really counts

Bring your thanks to God as a sacrifice, and keep your vows to the Most High.
PSALM 50:14 GOD'S WORD

The work done by a worshiper will have eternity in it.
A. W. TOZER

Thou who hast given Thine all in all for me, claim this life for Thine own, to be used, my Savior, every moment for Thee.
AVIS B. CHRISTIANSEN

What Matters Most to Me About
Worship

Worship involves awakening your consciousness to God, opening your heart and life to His purpose, connecting your mind to His truth, and lifting your voice in His praise. Take time here and now to worship God.

◎ *Because worship is a personal thing between you and God, song styles can affect your ability to join wholeheartedly in worship. How do you feel when worship songs are quiet and reserved? What picture of worship do you sense when songs are more spontaneous or exuberant? How do different song styles affect your worship?*

_____

_____

_____

_____

_____

_____

◎ *Your voice lifted in song is a wonderful gift of worship to God. What response have you received from others about your voice? How do these comments affect the way you sing when you worship God? What can you do when the comments of others makes singing your praise to God difficult?*

_____

_____

_____

_____

_____

_____

what
really
counts

◎ *The apostle Paul said Christians should offer their lives as living sacrifices of worship to God. What kind of a living sacrifice have you been? Are there areas of your life that need to change so that you can truly be God's living sacrifice? What has God been asking you to do that you've been putting off? What can you do to make those changes a reality?*

_____

_____

_____

_____

_____

_____

_____

◎ *A lifestyle of worship embodies a heart attitude that honors and glorifies God in everything. To truly be a living sacrifice, what ideas, dreams, goals, or relationships do you need to relinquish to honor God? What has to change in your life so that God takes first place?*

_____

_____

_____

_____

_____

_____

_____

_____

Give unto the LORD the glory due to His name;
worship the LORD in the beauty of holiness.
PSALM 29:2 NKJV

THE CHURCH

An Introduction

> The church then had peace throughout Judea, Galilee, and Samaria, and it grew in strength and numbers.
>
> ACTS 9:31 NLT

what really counts

The apostle Paul traveled to many cities on several missionary journeys to share his personal experiences with God with as many people as possible. Before he left each city, Paul made sure that those who believed in God had a place where they could meet and grow together in their faith. In some cities, widows let new converts meet in their homes. In other towns, believers met in caves or along the river's edge. Still other Christians used actual places of business for meeting places. Though lacking budgets and buildings, these gatherings were the forerunners of today's modern churches.

Paul made sure that each group of believers in each city had a leader to teach and guide the fledgling congregation. The Bible records that those who attended these early churches also actively looked for ways to help their pastor, giving the pastor more time for Bible study and prayer. These first-century Christians set an example for church involvement that still applies today.

Paul's personal example set another standard for both first-century churches and churches today. His willingness to share God's good news brought many into the church for the first time, so he urged believers in every church to follow his example and eagerly share their witness. Paul knew that outreach would help each church grow and strengthen each believer's faith. Paul's lessons still hold true today. Helping out in and reaching out from your church will bring growth, strength, and vitality to both your faith and your church.

Faith founded the church; hope has sustained it.
ARTHUR PENRHYN STANLEY

The Church

Inside Work

Through love serve one another.
GALATIANS 5:13 NKJV

There are days when every woman feels she has to do everything—housework, job, errands, shopping, cooking, etc. Though women are talented and able, sometimes it's nice to have a carryout person load your grocery bags into the car. It can be a plus to have assistance manhandling a washing machine up a flight of stairs. No woman would turn down someone's offer to help wash dishes, vacuum the floor, or scrub the toilet. Truly, many hands do make all work easier.

This truism applies to tasks in your church, too. Unfortunately, some church attendees believe their pastor, as a paid employee, is responsible for doing everything in the church. In addition to teaching the Bible, leading a Sunday school class or Bible study, and choosing the hymns for each worship service, the pastor is expected to serve on the church board and most of the committees, organize food and stewardship drives, and oversee youth and mission programs. The pastor might also have to visit shut-ins and hospital patients, write newsletter articles and devotionals, keep up with new widows, new babies, baptisms, weddings, funerals, membership roles, and be involved in the community as a shining example to all church constituents. Whew!

The early church did things differently. When folks complained that some widows were overlooked in a food distribution plan, early church leaders called the believers together and told them to choose wise, godly workers to look after the widows and make sure food was distributed fairly. In this way, the pastors could give more of their time to prayer and teaching the Bible. The early believers willingly did this, and thereby helped take some of the load from their leaders' shoulders.

Today many pastors' shoulders (and schedules) are overworked and overloaded. So why not offer your pastor a helping hand? Follow the first-century believers' example and put your God-given abilities to work in your church. Rather than expect your pastor to do everything, why not add your voice to the choir, teach a Sunday school class, or serve on the budget committee? Your pastor might need a helping hand to staff the nursery, paint the youth room, or decorate the sanctuary for the holidays. Truly, "many hands make light work" when it comes to your church. Look for ways to lighten your pastor's load. You'll find a blessing in such ministry and grow in your abilities, too.

The Church
Inside Work

What Matters Most...

◎ Serving with a willing heart.

◎ Loving one another enough to serve. Helping out shouldn't be a chore. Your love for others in your church should motivate you to help in whatever ways you can.

◎ Lightening your pastor's load. Though a paid employee, a pastor shouldn't carry the load of a church alone, or burnout will be just around the corner.

◎ Using your God-given talents. You've been blessed with abilities and talents. Use them to benefit your church.

What Doesn't Matter...

◎ What talents you have. Anything you can do to help in your church will lighten your pastor's load. Look for opportunities to serve.

◎ How much free time you have. Little moments here and there can always be used to help your church.

◎ Whether you attend a big or a small church. Regardless of size, all churches need all kinds of help.

◎ Your financial picture. Giving money isn't the only way to help your church. Your time and talents are also valuable.

◎ Your age, race, or size. There are areas of service for everyone in your church.

Focus Points...

As each one has received a special gift, employ it in serving one another as good stewards of the manifold grace of God.
1 PETER 4:10 NASB

I remind you to fan into flame the gift of God, which is in you.
2 TIMOTHY 1:6 NIV

Each person is given something to do that shows who God is: Everyone gets in on it, everyone benefits.
1 CORINTHIANS 12:7 MSG

Are you called to be a speaker? Then speak as though God himself were speaking through you. Are you called to help others? Do it with all the strength and energy that God supplies.
1 PETER 4:11 NLT

what really counts

The ministry of the church is a ministry of people. When a church lives, it lives because the people within are vital and active.

LLOYD CORY

The church exists to train its members through the practice of the presence of God to be servants of others.

WILLIAM ADAMS BROWN

The Church
Outside Witness

If anyone believes in me, rivers of living water will flow out from that person's heart.

JOHN 7:38 NCV

The Jordan River in the Middle East connects two bodies of water—to the north, the Sea of Galilee; to the south, the Dead Sea. The Sea of Galilee has many inlets and outlets and supports a viable fishing trade. The Dead Sea, however, has no outlet. The few streams that flow into it are heavy in minerals, turning this reservoir into a nauseating, oily body of water incapable of supporting any life or trade. The main difference between the two seas consists in outflow. When a body of water has many outlets, its water stays fresh and flowing. Cut off the outflow, however, and the water will stagnate, killing all life.

Churches can be a lot like these two seas. As both of the seas are filled with water, so all churches are filled with attendees, pastors, teachers, leaders, etc. And as both seas have inlets or ways to top off their water levels, church attendees find refilling through praise and worship, Bible study and prayer, sermons and special music. However, just as a sea will die for lack of an outflow, so also will a church die without an outlet. For a church to grow strong and vibrant, its members need to be committed to outflow—to sharing God's living water of faith and forgiveness with others.

A church can do this in many ways. Special programs for children, plays that present the Bible in unique ways, or music concerts are proven tools for reaching people with God's good news. Yet outflow in the church also needs the personal touch from individuals like you. When you find a good sale on something, you probably call a friend and tell her where to find the bargains. That's what outreach in the church and your witness is all about—your willingness to share with someone else the good that God is doing in your life.

To help your church grow strong, God wants you to be a part of your church's outflow. If you ask, He will provide you with opportunities uniquely fitted to your abilities so that you can be a part of that outflow, that witness, that sharing of your faith. Remember, every time you walk out the doors of your church, someone—a family member, friend, coworker, or hairstylist—could benefit from your faith story. For a vital faith, be a part of your church's outflow. Share God's good news with others.

The Church
Outside Witness

What Matters Most...

◉ Knowing that when outward movement is nonexistent, the eventual result is death, whether in a sea or in a church.

◉ Knowing that for a church to be strong and vibrant, its members need to be committed to corporate and personal outward movement.

◉ Knowing that God wants you to be a part of your church's outward movement and has a place of witness and sharing uniquely fitted to your abilities.

◉ Knowing that someone can benefit from your faith story whenever you are willing to share God's good news.

What Doesn't Matter...

◉ How big your church is. Willingness of heart to share God's good news makes the individual difference.

◉ How many special programs your church offers each month. Personally sharing with someone can have more impact than a special program.

◉ How many people you know.

◉ How comfortable you are sharing your faith. The first time you do anything—driving a car, baking cookies, changing diapers—it feels awkward.

Focus Points...

Jesus said to them again, "Peace to you! As the Father has sent Me, I also send you."
JOHN 20:21 NKJV

Before people can ask the Lord for help, they must believe in him; and before they can believe in him, they must hear about him; and for them to hear about the Lord, someone must tell them.
ROMANS 10:14 NCV

You shall be witnesses to Me in Jerusalem, and in all Judea and Samaria, and to the end of the earth.
ACTS 1:8 NKJV

Always be prepared to give an answer to everyone who asks you to give the reason for the hope that you have. But do this with gentleness and respect.
1 PETER 3:15 NIV

The holiest moment of the church service is the moment when God's people—strengthened by preaching and sacrament—go out of the church door into the world to be the church.

ERNEST SOUTHCOTT

If you want your neighbor to know what Christ will do for him, let the neighbor see what Christ has done for you.

HENRY WARD BEECHER

157

What Matters Most to Me About
The Church

A church is more than windows and doors, walls and floors. A church is made up of people—people who can help, people who can reach out, people just like you. Think about your place in the church as you consider these questions.

◉ *Write down some things that you do well. Can you cook well? Sing? Play drums? Can you teach? Paint? Don't discount your needfulness in your church just because your talent may be a bit different. Now list ways in which you can contribute these skills in your church. Commit to calling your church and offering your services.*

_____

_____

_____

_____

_____

_____

◉ *If people lack vision for involvement in the church, the flame of their gifts could sputter and die. Think about some older members in your church congregation. What are some ways you can encourage these older believers to fan the flame of their gifts in your church? Record your ideas here—then do one or two of them.*

_____

_____

_____

_____

_____

_____

Experience the darkness of an unlit room, remembering that a heart without God is a darkened heart. Record your feelings about that dark moment here. Now think about God's love for those outside the church with darkened hearts. In what ways could you help to bring the light of God's love to someone outside your church?

_____

_____

_____

_____

_____

_____

_____

_____

Identify one or two non-Christian friends. Is there something at your church that might interest them? Think back and remember the person(s) who introduced you to God. What were they like? What did they do? What did they say that influenced you? How can you follow their example when you're with your non-Christian friends?

_____

_____

_____

_____

_____

_____

_____

_____

The church is Christ's body, in which he speaks and acts, by which he fills everything with his presence.

EPHESIANS 1:23 MSG

WISDOM

An Introduction

> Teach the wise, and they will become even wiser; teach good people, and they will learn even more.
>
> PROVERBS 9:9 NCV

what really counts

Benjamin Franklin once published a periodical known as *Poor Richard's Almanac*, including in this publication wise sayings that have become a part of the American consciousness. While many of Franklin's axioms were jewels of truth and wisdom, other adages contradicted God's wisdom as found in the Bible. Though Franklin was well educated, his big blunder was his failure to recognize that there are two kinds of wisdom—worldly wisdom and God's wisdom. Heeding only worldly wisdom can cause you to follow wrong advice and make poor choices. Seeking and following God's wisdom, however, will bring about blessing, peace, and fulfillment.

Thirty years later, a wiser Ben Franklin addressed the Continental Congress as it stood at a crossroads.

Factions disagreed as to the direction the republic should go, calling for an immediate vote to settle the issue. Franklin, however, advised restraint, reminding the delegates that since God is actively involved in the lives of His people, the delegates should pause for prayer prior to acting upon any decision that would affect the republic.

Franklin's motion was carried. Thereafter, a prayer for God's wisdom was invoked at the beginning of each session. Within a few days, a compromise was approved—a compromise that is still in effect in Congress today, a compromise that came about only by taking time to seek God's wisdom in order to make a wise decision.

Worldly wisdom or God's wisdom? Hasty decisions or ones that have been worked through with prayer and forethought? Which wisdom will you choose?

WISDOM

Common sense suits itself to the ways of the world; wisdom tries to conform to the ways of heaven.

JOSEPH JOUBERT

Wisdom
Coffee-Klatch Wisdom

Even the foolishness of God is
wiser than human wisdom.

1 CORINTHIANS 1:25 NCV

**what
really
counts**

Put several ladies around a table with coffee and a lus-
cious, home-baked confection and you'll probably hear,
"Have a piece. It's been cut, so half the calories have leaked
out." Unfortunately, it's a proven fact of science: calories don't
leak out of broken cookies, cut cake, or mangled pie. It's just
too bad, but some words of wisdom aren't very wise.

Moses learned this lesson in a life-changing way. As the
adopted son of the king of Egypt, Moses was educated in all
Egypt's wisdom. However, some of that Egyptian wisdom
wasn't as wise as it seemed. Ancient Egyptian wisdom said
that the king was a god, that he could do no wrong, and that
the life of a slave was worthless. Regrettably, these ancient credos were as flawed as the broken-cookie calorie belief of the
coffee-klatch ladies. But Moses couldn't see that—that is,
until he had an experience with God. Attitudes, situations,
and circumstances that Moses had accepted as true or wise

were suddenly cast in a different light. Why? Because Moses found God's wisdom.

There are two types of wisdom—worldly wisdom and God's wisdom. While worldly, natural wisdom may contain gems of truth—the sun rises in the east and sets in the west—worldly wisdom can also be based on selfishness or greed, expressing itself today with thoughts like, *You've got to look out for number one* or *Everybody else is doing it.* However, God's wisdom is different. It comes from God's heart, it's wrapped in His nature, it protects you from pain, and it embodies only those things that are true, selfless, and just. The worldly wisdom that says everybody else is doing it can cause you to creep past the speed limit and fall into a costly ticket. God's wisdom says keep the speed limit (and your money!), reminding you to do only those things that honor and glorify Him—even when others don't. God's wisdom says don't worry about being number one. Instead, to find true fulfillment in life, make God number one and put the needs of others before your own.

Meeting God changed Moses' life because the experience changed Moses' source of wisdom. Your life, too, can change for the better if you change the source of your wisdom. Worldly wisdom will get you only so far. Seek God's wisdom by studying the Bible, and you'll find a life of blessing and joy.

Wisdom
Coffee-Klatch Wisdom

What Matters Most...

◎ Knowing that there are two kinds of wisdom in this world—worldly wisdom and God's wisdom.

◎ Recognizing that natural, worldly wisdom can sometimes be good but can sometimes be flawed.

◎ Understanding that God's wisdom originates in His nature and embodies those things that are true, selfless, and just.

◎ Remembering that you can find true fulfillment, blessing, joy, and satisfaction in life only when you follow God's wisdom.

What **Doesn't** Matter...

◎ The prevailing attitude of "me first."

◎ The credo that if it feels good, do it. It's another idea that's not as wise as the world would have you believe.

◎ Your past lessons in worldly wisdom.

◎ The opinions of others. Following God's wisdom will ultimately bring blessing, fulfillment, and joy—not foolishness.

◎ Your schedule. It takes time and energy to seek out God's wisdom in the Bible.

Focus Points...

Oh, the depth of the riches both of the wisdom and knowledge of God!
ROMANS 11:33 NKJV

True wisdom and real power belong to God; from him we learn how to live, and also what to live for.
JOB 12:13 MSG

Let the name of God be blessed forever and ever, for wisdom and power belong to Him.
DANIEL 2:20 NASB

The LORD gives wisdom; from His mouth come knowledge and understanding; He stores up sound wisdom for the upright.
PROVERBS 2:6–7 NKJV

what
really
counts

When followed, wisdom keeps us out of trouble by eliminating the possibility in the first place.

CHARLES STANLEY

When we realize that there is no hope of deliverance in human wisdom, or in human rectitude, or in anything that we can do ... this is the finest cure for spiritual degeneration.

OSWALD CHAMBERS

Wisdom
Making Wisdom Work

A wise person is hungry for truth,
while the fool feeds on trash.
PROVERBS 15:14 NLT

Nonstandard "small," "medium," and "large" size tags are a blot on every woman's shopping experience. Depending on the manufacturer, a "medium" can range anywhere from a size 10 to a size 14. To make a wise purchase, you have to not only find your size, but also take time to try the outfit on to make sure it fits. To make wise decisions in life, it's helpful to follow a similar principle: take time to test your decision, try it on, and see if it really works for you, or you could end up making a poor choice that won't fit God's best plan for your life.

Gehazi learned this lesson the hard way. God had healed a commander from the Aramaean army of his leprosy. The man wanted to reward God's prophet Elisha for this miracle, but Elisha refused, so the commander headed home. However, Gehazi, Elisha's servant, thought Elisha could have at least taken something from the man in return for his services. So Gehazi sneaked out of the house and ran after him. He told the commander a fib about some unexpected visitors who needed clothes and money. The man gladly offered twice what Gehazi asked for, and the servant hurried home to hide the goodies.

Elisha knew something sneaky was afoot. He found Gehazi and asked, "Where did you go?" Unfortunately, Gehazi compounded one bad decision with another, lying to Elisha about his whereabouts. If only Gehazi had been wise enough to take some time to think through the implications of lying—both to the commander and to Elisha—he would have remembered God's law forbids lying. But Gehazi's foolishness rushed him into a decision that left him leprous forever.

You, however, can avoid Gehazi's foolishness in the decision-making department with a few simple steps. First, preface any decision with prayer. If you need wisdom, you should ask God for it. Then ask yourself some questions. Will this decision please God? Will it hurt me? Will it hurt anyone else? Proceed with the decision only if you can honestly answer no to all three questions. Listing the good and bad things that could happen as a result of your decision can also help you find the wisdom you need to choose well. Don't be rushed into bad decisions that won't fit you or that won't fit God's best plan for your life. Take time to make wisdom work for you.

Wisdom
Making Wisdom Work

What Matters Most...

◎ Taking some time. Just as you would spend some time shopping for an outfit, take some time to make wise decisions.

◎ Praying and choosing the path you think might be right.

◎ Praying and looking at the situation from all angles when making a decision.

◎ Testing the fit of your decisions. Will God be pleased? Will it hurt you or someone else?

What Doesn't Matter...

◎ Time. Most decisions don't need to be rushed. Be wise. Take your time.

◎ Size. Wisdom works to fit decisions of all sizes. Take time to review a choice from all angles.

◎ Age. Though age brings the experience of years to the decision-making process, you can make good decisions at any age, provided you ask for God's wisdom every time.

◎ Failure. You've probably made a few wrong choices in your life. That doesn't mean you're doomed to make unwise decisions forever.

Focus Points...

You know what he wants; you know right from wrong because you have been taught his law.
ROMANS 2:18 NLT

Fools are headstrong and do what they like; wise people take advice.
PROVERBS 12:15 MSG

Wise men and women are always learning, always listening for fresh insights.
PROVERBS 18:15 MSG

If any of you needs wisdom to know what you should do, you should ask God, and he will give it to you.
JAMES 1:5 GOD'S WORD

what really counts

Show me the path where I should walk, O LORD; point out the right road for me to follow.
PSALM 25:4 NLT

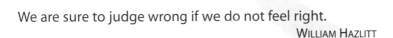

We are sure to judge wrong if we do not feel right.
WILLIAM HAZLITT

If we are ever in doubt about what to do, it is a good rule to ask ourselves what we shall wish on the morrow that we had done.
SIR JOHN LUBBOCK

What Matters Most to Me About
Wisdom

With two kinds of wisdom to choose from—worldly wisdom and God's wisdom—making snap decisions can result in costly mistakes. Reflect on wisdom and how to make it work for you as you consider these questions.

◎ *List some words of worldly wisdom that you might have heard growing up or that you've observed in your daily experience. Compare these credos with things you know about God. What conclusions can you draw about your personal experiences with the truth or falsehood of these worldly viewpoints?*

_____

_____

_____

_____

_____

_____

_____

◎ *Moses had to unlearn some worldly Egyptian wisdom when he met God. How has your experience with God changed your attitudes, viewpoints, or reactions to commonly held beliefs? What areas of your life still need to come into line with God's wisdom? What can you do to make these changes a reality?*

_____

_____

_____

_____

_____

_____

◎ *Record here an instance of a shopping expedition that resulted in a hasty purchase that you later regretted. What did you learn from that experience? What could you have done differently to avert that shopping disaster? How can you apply the lessons learned from this experience to your future decision making?*

_____

_____

_____

_____

_____

_____

_____

_____

◎ *Compose a prayer, asking God for wisdom. Ask Him to show you when you are relying on worldly wisdom instead of His wisdom. Ask Him to slow you down and help you take the time to make His wisdom work for you. Then remind yourself of this prayer when faced with any decision, trusting God to answer and give you the wisdom you need.*

_____

_____

_____

_____

_____

_____

_____

_____

Cry out for wisdom, and beg for understanding. Search for it like silver, and hunt for it like hidden treasure. Then you will understand respect for the LORD, and you will find that you know God.

PROVERBS 2:3–5 NCV

GOD'S WILL

An Introduction

> I will instruct you and teach you in the way you should go; I will guide you with My eye.
>
> PSALM 32:8 NKJV

what really counts

Following a formula can help you make a cake, fill a prescription, or fix a computer virus. However, finding the *right* formula is essential to guarantee that the cake will taste good, the prescription will be safe, and the computer fix will be a lasting one. The same is true when seeking the formula to finding and following God's will for your life. You may be faced with several options, and knowing what is or isn't God's will may be hard to discern.

So begin at the beginning. To find God's will for your life, start by reading the Bible. Because God made you, He knows the right formula for you to follow to have a wonderful life. He has promised to guide you, too, and to show you what He wants you to do. All you have to do is ask Him to direct you as you search the Bible for His will. God may also have a special mission for you to carry out for Him. To follow God's will in these instances, you need to be eager to do something or go somewhere unexpected whenever God calls you. A readiness to follow God's direction will always play an essential part in accomplishing God's will.

So what's the right formula to finding God's will for your life? Being ready, willing, and eager to do whatever God wants you to do. Indifference won't cut it. Passionately pursue God's will. Check out the Bible. You'll not only find direction, you'll also find Him.

> To know the will of God is the greatest knowledge! To do the will of God is the greatest achievement!
>
> GEORGE W. TRUETT

God's Will
What God Wants

What does the LORD require of you?
MICAH 6:8 NKJV

what really counts

What do you want to be? Where do you want to go? What are your goals and aspirations? Questions like these fill your mind, especially during life-changing moments like graduation from school, an impending career move, or a change in marital status. Yet if you are a child of God, God already has a direction figured out for your life. He has laid out good plans for you that will give you hope and ensure a good future for you. If you want to do what God wants, go where God wants, and choose those things that are a part of God's good will for your life, what should you do?

Why not begin at the beginning? To find out God's will for your life, pray. Ask God to show you His plan and purpose for your life. Then take a close look at the passages in the Bible that clearly tell you what God wants *all* His children to do and how He wants them to live. Start with the following four passages.

174

• "This is what the LORD your God wants you to do: Respect the LORD your God, and do what he has told you to do. Love him. Serve the LORD your God with your whole being, and obey the LORD's commands" (Deuteronomy 10:12–13 NCV). God's will for you is to *wholly serve God with respect, love, and obedience.*

• "What does the LORD require of you? To act justly and to love mercy and to walk humbly with your God" (Micah 6:8 NIV). God's will for you is to *live a life marked by justice, mercy, and humility.*

• " 'Love the Lord your God with all your heart, all your soul, all your strength, and all your mind.' Also, 'Love your neighbor as you love yourself' " (Luke 10:27 NCV). God's will for you is to *love God and others with everything you've got.*

• "In everything give thanks; for this is the will of God in Christ Jesus for you" (1 Thessalonians 5:18 NKJV). God's will for you is to *be thankful always—in good times and bad.*

There are many other passages in the Bible that can help you discern God's will for your life. Remember, God's plan for your life is a good one. If you want to know what God wants you to do, ask Him, search the Bible, and He will gladly show you.

God's Will
What God Wants

What Matters Most...

◎ Understanding that life involves changes that can affect your goals and the choices you make in your life's plan.

◎ Knowing that as a child of God, the choices you make should reflect the plan that God has for you.

◎ Recognizing that God's plan for your life is a good one, intended to bring you hope and a good future.

◎ Remembering that the best way to find out God's will for your life is to ask Him to reveal it to you.

◎ Discerning God's will through the Bible to find what God wants you to do and how He wants you to live.

What **Doesn't** Matter...

◎ What others say you should do. Though the advice of friends can be helpful, trust God to show you His will.

◎ Whether or not you're sure about your future. Only God knows the future; rely on Him to show you His plan.

◎ Your insecurities. Afraid of choosing something outside God's will? Ask Him to give you peace.

◎ Your unfamiliarity with the Bible. Make the study of the Bible a priority to find His sure will and way.

◎ Your current position or status. God has placed you where you are for His purpose. Seek His will and His way.

Focus Points...

It is God's will that your good lives should silence those who make foolish accusations against you.
1 PETER 2:15 NLT

It is God's will that you keep away from sexual sin as a mark of your devotion to him.
1 THESSALONIANS 4:3 GOD'S WORD

With all your heart you must do what God wants as people who are obeying Christ.
EPHESIANS 6:6 NCV

Be transformed by the renewing of your mind, that you may prove what is that good and acceptable and perfect will of God.
ROMANS 12:2 NKJV

what really counts

I was frustrated out of my mind, trying to figure out the will of God. I was doing everything but getting into the presence of God and asking Him to show me.

PAUL LITTLE

When we want to know God's will, there are three things which always concur: the inward impulse, the Word of God, and the trend of circumstances . . . Never act until these three things agree.

F. B. MEYER

God's Will
Be Prepared!

[Jesus] said, "Behold, I have come
to do Your will, O God."
HEBREWS 10:9 NKJV

Have you ever been in the middle of a recipe only to find
out you're missing an essential ingredient needed to complete
the yummy treat? Chefs know the scouting motto "Be prepared!" is always good advice to follow—especially if you
want to be a success in the kitchen.

Being prepared is also good advice when following God's
will for your life. You never know, but God may have a special
job or two for you to do. You'll need to be prepared to accomplish those tasks, just like Elisha's friend in 2 Kings 9.

God had been displeased with King Joram of Israel, so He
told the prophet Elisha to ask a friend to go on a dangerous
mission. God wanted Elisha's friend to go secretly to the camp
of Jehu and anoint him in God's name as the new king. Elisha
told his friend where to go and what to say, handed him a
flask of oil to use, and reminded him that as soon as he had
anointed Jehu king over Israel, he should run away without

178

delay. Just as the young man was getting ready to leave, Elisha reminded him to tuck his flowing robe into his belt. Elisha wanted his friend to be prepared to run long before he had to. Why? Maybe someone would have tried to grab the man's robe as he hurried into Jehu's presence. Maybe he would have tripped on his way out or caught his robe on a doorpost. Whatever the reason, Elisha knew that being prepared to do the job God sets before you is just as important as doing it.

It's the same way for you. A simple prayer can be the start of preparing yourself to do God's will. Ask God to get you ready for whatever He has in store for you. Then make yourself available to Him. When God called Samuel in the middle of the night, the young boy answered, "Speak, Lord! I'm listening." Isaiah responded to a vision of God asking for volunteers with a resounding "Here am I! Send me" (Isaiah 6:8 NKJV). You also need to be available and willing to be used when God calls. If you sense a tug on your heart to make a call, send a note, or even make a recipe, it could be God prompting you to do His will. Be ready, willing, and able. Be prepared to do God's will.

God's Will
Be Prepared!

What Matters Most...

- Recognizing that God may have special tasks He wants you to do for Him.

- Preparing yourself through prayer so that you're ready whenever God calls you for a special task.

- Remembering that God uses willing, available people to do His will. Be prepared, willing, and available for God to use you.

- Being aware of God's promptings and recognizing them as God's call to use you to work out His will.

- Being prepared to do God's will.

What **Doesn't** Matter...

- How well you follow a recipe. What counts is following God's will. Be prepared to recognize His will and do it quickly.

- How often God has used you before. God's will for you may include many tasks or just one. Let God decide.

- How many talents you have.

- How qualified you feel you are to do God's will. Feelings are irrelevant. God promises you'll have what you need to do what He wants.

Focus Points...

Teach me to do your will, for you are my God. May your gracious Spirit lead me forward on a firm footing.
PSALM 143:10 NLT

Prepare the way for the LORD; make straight in the wilderness a highway for our God.
ISAIAH 40:3 NIV

Be a vessel for honor, sanctified and useful for the Master, prepared for every good work.
2 TIMOTHY 2:21 NKJV

Be ready at all times, and tell people what they need to do. Tell them when they are wrong. Encourage them with great patience and careful teaching.
2 TIMOTHY 4:2 NCV

what really counts

I heard the voice of the Lord, saying: "Whom shall I send, and who will go for Us?" Then I said, "Here am I! Send me."
ISAIAH 6:8 NKJV

True devotion to God consists in doing all His will precisely at the time, in the situation, and under the circumstances in which He has placed us.

FRANÇOIS FÉNELON

Get into the habit of saying, "Speak, Lord," and life will become a romance.

OSWALD CHAMBERS

181

What Matters Most to Me About
God's Will

God wants you to follow His will for your life so that your life will honor and glorify Him. Reflect on God's will for your life as you think about these questions.

◎ *Searching the Bible can help you find God's will for your life. A piece of God's will for every believer is that you obey His laws for living. What can you derive about God's will for your life from the Ten Commandments (Exodus 20)?*

_____

_____

_____

_____

_____

_____

_____

_____

◎ *Sometimes the best way to know God's will is to let go of your own ideas and let God have His way, even when it may not seem easy or pleasant. Record some of the unpleasant or hard things you might have to do to follow God's will. Commit yourself to follow through on these things if God wills it.*

_____

_____

_____

_____

_____

_____

_____

what
really
counts

Think about a time when you felt a heart-tug to do something, go somewhere, say something, or call someone. What did you do? Recognizing that a heart-tug could be God's way of getting you to do His will, what will you have to do to be better prepared to act on His heart-tugs in the future?

_____

_____

_____

_____

_____

_____

_____

_____

_____

If you are a child of God, He already has a plan and a will for your life. How do you feel knowing that God's plan may or may not be the plan and will you have for your life? God wants only what's best for you. How does this knowledge affect your willingness to passionately pursue God's will?

_____

_____

_____

_____

_____

_____

_____

_____

_____

The plans of the LORD stand firm forever, the purposes of his heart through all generations.
PSALM 33:11 NIV

PEACE AND HAPPINESS
An Introduction

> You shall go out with joy, and be led out with peace; the mountains and the hills shall break forth into singing before you.
>
> ISAIAH 55:12 NKJV

what really counts

A small child ran into the kitchen, calling, "Mom! Mom! The kitty's boiling over!" Together mother and child rushed to the family pet's side. There in a pool of warm sunlight the furry creature lay—stretched out, eyes closed, barely moving. To the child's relief, Mom explained that the sound of the cat's purr was not a sign of overheating, but rather a peaceful response to a happy situation, like someone humming a tune. As the family pet basked in the sunlight, the little one skipped off happily, humming a childlike version of the kitty's peaceful purr.

Living in peace is something pets and people prefer to do. However, a pet's peaceful purr can be broken by an unexpected event, a shouted disagreement, or a nearby scuffle. Peace between people can be broken by these things, too. Yet God has a plan for restoring peace to broken relationships. The Bible gives suggestions to help patch things up and bring back the peaceful purr of personal fellowship and friendship.

Peace also has an emotional assistant, a sidekick, a helper. To keep peace in your heart and relationships, you need to find God's joy. Though happiness can slip away as quickly as a skittish cat, your heart can resonate with a peaceful purr whenever God's joy grabs hold of your inner spirit. So bask in the sunlight of God. Experience His deep-down peace and joy. Then stretch out with a purr, and share that peace and joy with others.

> Lord, make me an instrument of Your peace! Where there is hatred, let me sow love ... where there is darkness, light; where there is sadness, joy.
> SAINT FRANCIS OF ASSISI

Peace and Happiness

Peace Work

> Remember to live peaceably
> with each other.
>
> 1 THESSALONIANS 5:13 NLT

what really counts

Mention the word *peace,* and women visibly relax. Minds wander to images of scented bubble baths or hammocks swaying in the breeze. Hearts everywhere long for peace, but sometimes broken relationships can make it difficult to keep peace alive and well. Because peace is an aspect of God's nature, He wants you to experience this harmony, security, and contentment with your friends, family, and other believers. To restore a sense of peace to broken relationships, talk to God first about the friction between you and someone else. Vent. Explain. Get it out of your system, but direct your comments to God alone. Only His shoulders are broad enough to carry that load. Then follow these God-given guidelines to work peace back into your relationship.

Be willing to take the first step to restore peace. If you know there's a problem in a relationship, "first go away and make peace with that person" (Matthew 5:24 GOD'S WORD).

Open the door to peace by saying, "You're too important to me to let this come between us."

Try to understand the other person's feelings. The Bible puts it this way: "Be agreeable, be sympathetic, be loving, be compassionate, be humble. That goes for all of you, no exceptions. No retaliation. No sharp-tongued sarcasm" (1 Peter 3:8–9 MSG).

Admit your part in the peace-breaking. Though you might be terribly hurt because of someone's actions, remember, it always takes two to create friction. "How can you think of saying, 'Friend, let me help you get rid of that speck in your eye,' when you can't see past the log in your own eye?" (Matthew 7:4 NLT). Be honest; give up your self-centeredness to restore peace.

Look for ways to fix the peace, not fix the blame. The psalmist said, "Do good. Look for peace and work for it" (Psalm 34:14 NCV).

Focus on a restored, peaceful relationship, rather than on the problem that exists between you. You can disagree with each other, but you don't have to be disagreeable about it. Settle the relationship between you, remembering that God forgave you and restored your relationship. You can do the same.

Remember, God wants His children to live in peace. It's up to you to do the peace work.

Peace and Happiness
Peace Work

What Matters Most...

◎ Knowing that peace is an aspect of God's nature and a necessary part of your spiritual growth and life.

◎ Recognizing the importance of restoring God's peace to broken relationships.

◎ Being willing to actively pursue peace in all relationships, whether whole or broken.

◎ Doing the work of peace by following God's example and settling relationships with others. Resolve your conflicts so that you can follow God's directive: live in peace.

What **Doesn't** Matter...

◎ How tough keeping the peace can be.

◎ Who broke the peace in the first place. Placing blame doesn't rebuild peaceful relationships.

◎ What they said; what you said; what others say. Broken relationships need the oil of peace. Ask for God's help.

◎ How silly you think the other person's viewpoint is. Try to be sympathetic anyway. Seek understanding.

◎ How disagreeable some people can be. You, too, have probably been disagreeable.

Focus Points...

The LORD will give strength to His people; the LORD will bless His people with peace.
PSALM 29:11 NKJV

When people live so that they please the LORD, even their enemies will make peace with them.
PROVERBS 16:7 NCV

You are joined together with peace through the Spirit, so make every effort to continue together in this way.
EPHESIANS 4:3 NCV

Do your part to live in peace with everyone, as much as possible.
ROMANS 12:18 NLT

what really counts

The fruit of righteousness is sown in peace by those who make peace.
JAMES 3:18 NKJV

When quarrels happen, we should be willing to be friends again upon any terms; peace and love are such valuable jewels that we can scarcely buy them too dearly.

MATTHEW HENRY

Sowing seeds of peace is like sowing beans. You don't know why it works; you just know it does. Seeds are planted, and topsoils of hurt are shoved away.

MAX LUCADO

Peace and Happiness
Holy Happiness

Rejoice in the Lord always. Again
I will say, rejoice!

PHILIPPIANS 4:4 NKJV

She was late for a meeting. Stumbling into heels that matched her silk suit, she remembered a childhood command: "Always use the bathroom before leaving the house!" Located in a former closet, her tiny powder room barely allowed an occupant room enough to enter and exit, yet she wiggled in and carefully arranged herself so as not to wrinkle her suit. As she struggled to pull her panty hose back into place, the flush level *kersplooshed* like always. But then something went wrong. As she carefully tugged her panty hose almost to knee height, the woman realized the toilet was clogged; the bowl was almost full. She wheeled about, snatched her silk suit's skirt in her teeth, yanked her suit sleeves as high as they'd go, and tore the lid off the back of the toilet. But she was too late. Even as she groped for the interior flushing mechanism, the water in the toilet bowl began to splash over onto her knock-kneed, panty hose–constricted form. *This can't be happening*, she thought. And then she began to laugh, realizing how hilarious her useless struggling in that tiny powder room would have appeared to a bystander. Was she happy that the wetting down would make her even later for her meeting? No. But was she joyful? Oh, yes!

How can that be? Simple, really. Happiness and joy are different things. Happiness is tied to circumstance. Unfortunately, if circumstances change, happiness can evaporate. For example, you might be happy with a dress purchase because of its fit or color—happy, that is, until you see another woman wearing the exact same outfit. When that happens, your happiness vanishes.

But joy is different. Joy is possible even in horrible situations. Habakkuk said if he had no food, no crops, no animals in the barnyard, "I will joy in the God of my salvation" (Habakkuk 3:18 NKJV). Habakkuk knew joy wasn't linked to outside circumstance. It's a deeper, holier type of happiness. Joy comes from growing up in God, from sensing His presence in your life, from bearing His fruit of the Spirit. Such joy is unshakable. It bubbles up from the inside, overflows from your heart, and splashes onto others.

No, there's nothing wrong with looking for happiness in life, but don't stop there. Go deeper in your relationship with God. Ask Him to fill you with the lasting, splashing Holy Spirit fruit of joy. And then—rejoice.

Peace and Happiness
Holy Happiness

What Matters Most...

- Recognizing the difference between happiness and joy. One is fleeting; the other, lasting.

- Remembering that joy comes from growing up in God, from sensing His presence in your life, from bearing His fruit of the Spirit.

- Understanding that the joy that comes from God is strong and unshakable.

- Knowing that joy can bubble up from your heart and not only bless you, but also splash and overflow onto others.

What **Doesn't** Matter...

- How happy you have or haven't been in the past. Happiness comes and goes. Ask God to teach you more about Himself, to fill you full of His Holy Spirit, and thereby receive His constant joy.

- What kind of day you're having. Good and bad days happen to everyone.

- That you don't feel joyful right now. Feelings come and go, just as happiness does.

- That you've pursued happiness and have often come up short. Remember, God promises you hope, joy, and peace *when you trust Him.*

Focus Points...

In the kingdom of God, eating and drinking are not important. The important things are living right with God, peace, and joy in the Holy Spirit.
ROMANS 14:17 NCV

God will yet fill your mouth with laughter and your lips with shouts of joy.
JOB 8:21 NCV

You will show me the path of life; in Your presence is fullness of joy; at Your right hand are pleasures forevermore.
PSALM 16:11 NKJV

You make the path of life known to me. In your presence there is complete joy.
ACTS 2:28 GOD'S WORD

what really counts

The LORD has done great things for us, and we are filled with joy.
PSALM 126:3 NIV

A joyful heart is the normal result of a heart burning with love. Never let anything so fill you with sorrow as to make you forget the joy of Christ Risen.

MOTHER TERESA

The surest mark of a Christian is not faith, or even love, but joy.

SAMUEL M. SHOEMAKER

What Matters Most to Me About
Peace and Happiness

Peace and holy happiness bring blessing to your heart. As you record your answers below, don't forget to look for ways to splash peace and joy on others, too.

◉ *God does not turn away from you whenever you go to Him for the restoration of peace in your relationship with Him. What does God's reaction tell you about your responses to friends, family, or church members who may have hurt you? How can you show God's peace to them?*

_____

_____

_____

_____

_____

_____

◉ *Because God is the source of all peace and joy, you can have a peaceful, joyful life only if you have a personal connection with Him. Write a prayer asking God to bless your life with His presence and peace. Then add a word of thanks, in advance, for the joy that God will send your way.*

_____

_____

_____

_____

_____

_____

○ *Think about a time when your heart was bursting with joy. Maybe that time is today. Write a prayer, poem, or song of joy and thanksgiving to God. He is worthy of your praise.*

_____

_____

_____

_____

_____

_____

_____

_____

_____

○ *The hard things of life don't need to affect your joy. Record here some of the hard things in your life right now. Alongside them, make a list of the good, joyful things in your life. God is faithful, good, loving—regardless of your situation. Rejoice in these remembrances.*

_____

_____

_____

_____

_____

_____

_____

_____

_____

The peace of God, which transcends all understanding, will guard your hearts and your minds in Christ Jesus.

PHILIPPIANS 4:7 NIV

CHARACTER

An Introduction

> Grow in the grace and knowledge of our Lord and Savior Jesus Christ.
>
> 2 PETER 3:18 NKJV

what really counts

Researchers contend that dreams, and the items in dreams, tell a lot about a person. They say if you dream about running late for an appointment or arriving at a place and not knowing how to find the room where you are supposed to be, it's likely that you're under stress during your waking hours. If your dreams are filled with thoughts of food you could be either at ease and relaxed or on a strict diet regimen while awake. Dreams about houses, however, usually indicate more personal issues because life is lived within the walls of a home.

Dream metaphors can apply to spiritual things, too, for the Bible often refers to your body as your earthly home. Just as different rooms in a home are used for different purposes, so you can associate each room in a home with a different aspect of discipleship. For example, as a woman you've already learned about patience waiting for the bathroom—in public places and at home—but you can also learn about cleanliness of heart from your laundry room, about acceptance when opening your front door. Your living room can be a place to share a kind word, an overstuffed closet might mirror bad attitudes, and your kitchen can sometimes be a place of difficulty—especially when you burn dinner.

When God cleansed your heart, He made it His home. So walk through the rooms of your home and your heart, letting each become a place of growth and discipleship.

> Salvation is just the beginning of what God wants to do for you.
>
> GEORGE SWEETING

Character
All Are Welcome

Jews have no dealings with Samaritans.

JOHN 4:9 NKJV

The doorbell rings. You glance quickly in the mirror to make sure you look fabulous (as always!), sweep the front door open, and welcome your guests with a "Come on in." Such a warm welcome is not only the mark of a good host, but also a seal of acceptance passed from one to another.

Accepting one another is not only commended but also commanded in the Bible. However, people often choose to highlight their differences, to discriminate between folks rather than offer the warm welcome of acceptance to all. This problem of favoritism often starts in childhood. Kids want to be well liked, so they ally themselves with other children who are well accepted. Unfortunately, adults often do the same thing, making alliances with the "beautiful" people but avoiding those who don't seem to be able to elevate their social status.

The Bible indicates that this human failing toward favoritism, discrimination, and prejudice is common. Peter adamantly refused to go to Cornelius's house because of

Peter's prejudice against non-Jews. Euodia and Syntyche squabbled between themselves in the Philippian church because each one believed she was better than the other. The woman at the well was amazed that Jesus would speak to her, not only because she was a Samaritan, but also because she had a checkered past. Even the early church esteemed the rich while treating the poor as second-class citizens. James asked, "Doesn't this discrimination show that you are guided by wrong motives?" (James 2:4 NLT).

Though you may have customs different from another believer's, may live in different parts of town, may earn more or less than another Christian, may be more sophisticated or a bit rougher around the edges than another child of God, all believers have the same heavenly Father. In Him there are no barriers of race, age, weight, gender, mental capacity, on economic or social standing. Measuring someone's significance based on achievement, status, or sophistication corresponds to making a value judgment about a person's worth. Because God values everyone equally—rich or poor, convict or congressman—God expects His children to also value everyone equally. So be God's messenger of acceptance. Open the door of your heart to another Christian who might be a bit different from you. You might just experience acceptance in a brand-new way and learn how pleasant it can be when brothers and sisters in faith live together in harmony.

Character
All Are Welcome

What Matters Most...

◎ Remembering that God wants His children to get along, love one another, and value one another equally.

◎ Understanding that the desire to be seen with the "right" people is a sign of impure motives.

◎ Acknowledging that playing favorites is a common human failing that God wants you to avoid at all times.

◎ Learning how good and pleasant it can be to live in welcoming acceptance and harmony with all God's children.

What **Doesn't** Matter...

◎ Your achievements. Human successes don't impress God. Your willingness to value what He values is what matters.

◎ Your social standing. Any one can be God's channel.

◎ Your bank account. Often the poor are richer in spiritual things because of their reliance on God.

◎ Where you live, work, or worship. You're God's child and can offer His gift of acceptance to anyone, anytime.

◎ Your family background. Regardless of your background, be God's ambassador of acceptance.

Focus Points...

Are we not all children of the same Father? Are we not all created by the same God? Then why are we faithless to each other?
MALACHI 2:10 NLT

The rich and the poor have this in common, the LORD is the maker of them all.
PROVERBS 22:2 NKJV

The LORD your God is God of gods and Lord of lords, the great God, mighty and awesome, who shows no partiality.
DEUTERONOMY 10:17 NKJV

Live in harmony with each other. Don't try to act important, but enjoy the company of ordinary people. And don't think you know it all!
ROMANS 12:16 NLT

what
really
counts

The issue is not whether the distinction is made over economic, social, educational, physical, spiritual, or health concerns or differences. The issue is that our motives for making the distinction are immediately called into question because favoritism is sin.

GARY SMALLEY AND JOHN TRENT

God's blessing is bestowed in fullness and power only when His people are truly together. Unity, harmony, and togetherness in the church equals courage, faith, miracles, and new believers.

BILL MCCARTNEY

Character
A Little "Let"

Keep your heart with all diligence,
for out of it spring the issues of life.
PROVERBS 4:23 NKJV

It's there. Every home has one. It's that overstuffed closet located by the front door, tucked into a bedroom, or down a back hall. If your home should wiggle ever so slightly under a shuddering tremor of the earth's crust or lean imperceptibly from the constant push of a strong wind, the door to that chock-full closet would burst open, spewing its contents everywhere, making a mess of everything.

Attitudes fill your heart like stuff fills a closet. All attitudes—whether positive or negative—are inward thoughts or feelings that express themselves in outward behavior. Attitudes affect your outlook on life and have an impact on the way you live. Unfortunately, negative attitudes sometimes find their way deep into your heart, crowding out positive ones. Those negative feelings sit there, piling on top of other similar attitudes, until your spirit becomes one big, negative container overstuffed with contempt, disrespect, bitterness, distrust, stubbornness, indifference, pride, jealousy, partiality, and rebellion. You may not immediately notice the effect of a negative attitude on your spirit. But it's there; its growth is slow and subtle. It colors every part of your life and touches those around you. And, like an overstuffed closet, eventually one little situation, one small word or circumstance, can blow the door of a negative spirit wide open, spewing angry words and bitterness everywhere.

Regrettably, negative attitudes got the better of Euodia and Syntyche, two ladies from Philippi. Their negative behavior had become so out of control, it became public. In fact, Paul heard about it in prison hundreds of miles away. He knew how destructive negative attitudes could be in a believer's life and understood that growth in Christian discipleship involves filling your heart with good attitudes. So Paul asked the Philippians to help these women resolve their negative differences so that they could continue helping to spread the good news about Jesus.

Paul's directives for these Philippian believers highlight an important spiritual principle: negative attitudes are inconsistent with Christianity. If you want to grow closer to God, the Bible urges you to replace negative attitudes with positive ones like love, forgiveness, helpfulness, hospitality, kindness, patience, humility, unselfishness, gentleness, courage, and joy. These positive attitudes are parts of God's character. And they're yours for a little "let": let God touch your heart through prayer; let go of your negative attitudes; and let the positive facets of God's character grow in you as you grow in discipleship.

Character
A Little "Let"

What Matters Most...

◎ Remembering negative attitudes can fill a heart just as full as positive ones.

◎ Knowing that negative attitudes are inconsistent with Christian growth and discipleship.

◎ Realizing that both positive and negative attitudes take many forms and affect your life in many ways.

◎ Replacing any negative attitudes with positive ones that are aspects of God's character.

What **Doesn't** Matter...

◎ What circumstances you face right now. You can always choose to be positive, even in negative situations.

◎ Other folks' attitudes. The only pressure you need to give in to is God's. Have the same attitude He has.

◎ How many negative attitudes are hiding in your heart. God wants His best for you. Replace those negatives with His positives.

◎ How old you are. Negative attitudes can creep into your life at any age. Keep a watchful eye on your heart.

◎ That you're a good person. Good people can harbor bad feelings. Anytime you find a negative attitude, get rid of it.

Focus Points...

Have the same attitude that Christ Jesus had. Although he was in the form of God and equal with God, he did not take advantage of this equality. Instead, he emptied himself by taking on the form of a servant, by becoming like other humans, by having a human appearance. He humbled himself by becoming obedient to the point of death, death on a cross.
PHILIPPIANS 2:5–8 GOD'S WORD

Those who say they live in God should live their lives as Christ did.
1 JOHN 2:6 NLT

There must be a spiritual renewal of your thoughts and attitudes.
EPHESIANS 4:23 NLT

what really counts

Pride will destroy a person; a proud attitude leads to ruin.
PROVERBS 16:18 NCV

If you wish to travel far and fast, travel light. Take off all your envies, jealousies, unforgiveness, selfishness, and fears.
GLENN CLARK

There is little difference in people, but that little difference makes a big difference. That little difference is attitude. The big difference is whether it is positive or negative.
CLEMENT STONE

Character
A Clean Slate

> What joy for those whose disobedience is forgiven, whose sins are put out of sight.
>
> ROMANS 4:7 NLT

Chances are, you begin and end your day in your bedroom. Every morning as you pry your eyes open and grope for the alarm clock, a new day beckons. And every evening as you crawl between the covers, you end the day by closing your eyes. Your bedroom becomes a place to start and finish each day with a clean slate. In essence, your bedroom becomes a mirror of forgiveness.

Forgiveness is an act of loving-kindness that frees a person from guilt and its consequences in order to restore a broken, personal relationship. Because God is forgiving, gracious, and compassionate, slow to get angry, and overflowing in love and kindness, He "does not treat us as our sins deserve or repay us according to our iniquities" (Psalm 103:10 NIV). Instead, God offers you a clean slate. Whenever you pray and ask for His forgiveness, God will wipe away the consequences of your mistakes and failings and restore you to a full, loving relationship with Him.

Since God has extended the gift of forgiveness to you, He wants you, too, to pass it along to others. Jesus told the story of a servant who owed a king a large sum of money. The servant couldn't repay the sum immediately and begged for mercy, promising to repay the king every penny. The king felt pity for the man and mercifully forgave the whole debt. But the servant went to a friend who owed him a small sum. He grabbed him by the throat and demanded instant payment. When the other fellow couldn't pay, the unforgiving servant had him thrown into prison. The king heard about this and was angry. "I forgave you that tremendous debt because you pleaded with me," the king said. "Shouldn't you have had mercy just as I had mercy on you?"

Jesus' story is clear. If you wish to grow closer to God, forgiveness needs to be a part of your spiritual repertoire. Because everyone needs to be forgiven for something at some time, God wants you to forgive others, just as you have been forgiven. You may even need to forgive yourself for a weakness, mistake, or poor decision. When you crawl out of bed in the morning or slip between the covers at night, remember that prayers for forgiveness—your forgiveness of others and God's forgiveness of you—can wipe the slate of your heart clean and give your faith a fresh start.

Character
A Clean Slate

What Matters Most...

◎ Forgiveness. It is a part of God's nature; He is unwilling to withhold forgiveness if you ask for it.

◎ Forgiveness. God offers it to everyone.

◎ Forgiveness. It is a sign of love. Forgiveness touches your heart with God's love and extends His love to others, too.

◎ Forgiveness. It is necessary to restore a broken relationship.

◎ Forgiveness. It is something you should give yourself. You will make mistakes. God forgives you; you should forgive yourself, too.

What Doesn't Matter...

◎ How many times you've been forgiven. God doesn't keep a scorecard of forgiveness. God forgives and forgets.

◎ How many times you've forgiven someone else. God's forgiveness is limitless; yours should be, too.

◎ Whether or not you've been forgiven by others. If you need to set the matter right, do so. Then forgive and move on.

◎ When you ask for forgiveness. God will always hear your prayer for forgiveness—and answer it with a resounding "YES."

Focus Points...

If we confess our sins, He is faithful and just to forgive us our sins and to cleanse us from all unrighteousness.
1 JOHN 1:9 NKJV

I will forgive their wrongdoings, and I will never again remember their sins.
HEBREWS 8:12 NLT

You must make allowance for each other's faults and forgive the person who offends you. Remember, the Lord forgave you, so you must forgive others.
COLOSSIANS 3:13 NLT

If you do not forgive, neither will your Father in heaven forgive your trespasses.
MARK 11:26 NKJV

what really counts

Forgiveness is a stunning principle, your ticket out of hate and fear and chaos. I know what regret feels like; I've earned my credentials. But I also know what forgiveness feels like, because God has so graciously forgiven me.
BARBARA JOHNSON

Forgiveness is not an emotion . . . Forgiveness is an act of the will, and the will can function regardless of the temperature of the heart.
CORRIE TEN BOOM

Character
Burned Toast

We can rejoice, too, when we run into problems and trials, for we know that they are good for us.
ROMANS 5:3 NLT

Troublesome situations can often happen in the kitchen. While there's nothing like a kitchen for delicious scents, wonderful flavors, and good fellowship, there's also nothing like a kitchen for overcooked dinners, burned toast, and blaring smoke alarms. Things break. Food spoils. Stuff happens in the kitchen—and in life, too.

Ruth knew this well. She had married into a fine Jewish family that had moved into her neighborhood in Moab. Things went well for several years, but when Ruth and her mother-in-law, Naomi, were unexpectedly widowed, Naomi and Ruth decided to move back to Israel. However, life became extremely difficult. Ruth was barely able to find enough leftover pieces of grain in the already harvested fields to feed herself and her mother-in-law. Yet Ruth had promised to stay with Naomi, to take care of her and become one of God's people. Ruth stayed true to her word and true to her faith in God, trusting that He would somehow either remove her difficulties or make them easier to bear.

And God did. He gave Ruth a new husband. He gave Naomi grandchildren and laughter after years of sadness. God can do the same for you, too. He knows how you feel. He sees your heart. He understands the pain, confusion, and concern that troubles can bring. Yet, because you are God's child, He promises to help you take the difficulties of life and find goodness in them just as you can find a wonderful glass of lemonade in the sourest of lemons. How? By helping you focus the eyes of your faith on Him.

Discipleship involves learning to lean on God whenever difficulties come. So let your next kitchen disaster be a trial run for stretching your faith. As you silence the smoke alarm or toss the ruined meal, let prayer become a first response, not a last resort. Ask God for a good resolution to this minor difficulty. Then believe God's promise that He has planned a good future for you full of hope. Remember His past faithfulnesses to you and find reassurance of His willingness to come to your aid again. God is with you, God loves you, and "is good to everyone and has compassion for everything that he has made" (Psalm 145:9 GOD'S WORD). Ask God to take care of your difficulties—burned toast or worse—focusing the eyes of your faith not on your problems but on the problem solver—God Himself.

Character
Burned Toast

What Matters Most...

◎ Remembering that difficulties are a part of life, both in the kitchen and out of it.

◎ Staying true to your commitment to God, trusting Him to either remove your difficulties or make them easier to bear.

◎ Believing that God can use difficulties to teach you to lean on Him for strength whenever troubles come.

◎ Focusing the eyes of your faith not on the problems around you, but on God, your problem solver.

What **Doesn't** Matter...

◎ How well you cook. Whether you're a chef or a microwave maven, you'll have a difficulty or two in life. Let God be your resource.

◎ How many large or small disasters you face each day. Turn all difficulties over to God for His oversight and care.

◎ Your faulty memory. Keep a running list of God's faithfulnesses to you. Refer to this list when difficulties arise.

◎ That stuff happens. God is always there for you in any difficulty. Ask Him to help turn your lemons into lemonade.

Focus Points...

I take limitations in stride, and with good cheer, these limitations that cut me down to size—abuse, accidents, opposition, bad breaks. I just let Christ take over!
2 Corinthians 12:10 msg

He does not ignore those in trouble. He doesn't hide from them but listens when they call out to him.
Psalm 22:24 ncv

Consider it a sheer gift, friends, when tests and challenges come at you from all sides. You know that under pressure, your faith-life is forced into the open and shows its true colors. So don't try to get out of anything prematurely. Let it do its work so you become mature.
James 1:2–4 msg

what really counts

God can summon unexpected reinforcements at any moment to help His people. Believe that He is between you and your difficulty, and what troubles you will flee before Him, as clouds in the wind.

F. B. Meyer

Kites rise not *with* the wind, but *against* it. So it is with us. We will not rise to patience and maturity unless we ascend against trials.

Elisa Morgan

Character
In the Company of Kings

> I am the LORD, who exercises kindness, justice and righteousness on earth, for in these I delight.
>
> JEREMIAH 9:24 NIV

Your great-grandmother might have called it the "front room" or the "parlor." Today, it's the "living room"—that area of your home in which guests are most welcome. A visitor to your home would rarely be invited into your bedroom or bathroom for a chat. Instead, your living room is the place where you can show kindness to guests with polite conversation, a shared cup of coffee, or a moment's rest in a comfortable chair.

Kindness is one of the traits of faith that are "the fruit of the Spirit" (Galatians 5:22 NKJV). When God's love fills your heart, kindness is what flows out to others. It is the behavior and mind-set that always look out for the good of someone else. Even when you have to enforce a rule, stand firm for the truth, or make a tough decision that can affect others, kindness keeps you from giving in to meanness or spite. Kindness can help you stand firm without forcing others to break.

Kindness continues, too. You don't stop being kind to someone just because you've already been kind for two or three weeks. As long as God's love flows through your heart, kindness resides there.

King David learned the lesson of kindness well, especially when it came to his childhood friend Jonathan. The boys had pledged their friendship to each other, promising to be kind not only to each other, but also to each other's families. When Saul and Jonathan were both killed in battle, David remembered his promise to his childhood friend. He learned that Jonathan had a son who was crippled in both feet. King David brought the boy to his palace and said, "I want to show kindness to you for the sake of your father, Jonathan. I will restore to you all the land that belonged to your grandfather Saul, and you will always eat at my table."

Though kindness may be considered by some to be a weakness, in God's economy, godly compassion for others is a sign of greatness. To look beyond yourself and see and minister to the needs of others places you in the company of kings like David. Your acts of kindness, whether shared in your living room or in a classroom, office, homeless shelter, hospital, or any other public place, mark you as one who knows God, loves God, and is growing in discipleship with God.

Character
In the Company of Kings

What Matters Most...

◎ Kindness. It's a fruit of the Holy Spirit. When God's Spirit flows through you, you can spread kindness to others.

◎ Kindness. It's an emotional governor. When godly kindness tempers your actions, you're less apt to be spiteful or mean-spirited.

◎ Kindness. It's long-lasting. You don't put a stop sign on kindness. It's a behavior that keeps on giving.

◎ Kindness. It's a sign of greatness. It takes true godliness to show kindness to hurtful people.

◎ Kindness. It illustrates growing faith.

What **Doesn't** Matter...

◎ Your social status.

◎ Your education. It doesn't take six college degrees to learn to be kind. Treat others the way you'd like to be treated.

◎ Your age. David and Jonathan showed kindness to each other when they were kids. You're never too young—or old—to be kind.

◎ Your personality type. Shy or outgoing, quiet or brassy, there's always a way for you to show kindness to others.

◎ Your nationality. God's ultimate kindness—salvation—is offered to everyone.

Focus Points...

This is what the LORD Almighty says: Judge fairly and honestly, and show mercy and kindness to one another.
ZECHARIAH 7:9 NLT

Add to your faith virtue, to virtue knowledge, to knowledge self-control, to self-control perseverance, to perseverance godliness, to godliness brotherly kindness, and to brotherly kindness love.
2 PETER 1:5–7 NKJV

Be kind to one another, tenderhearted, forgiving one another, even as God in Christ forgave you.
EPHESIANS 4:32 NKJV

To sum up, all of you be harmonious, sympathetic, brotherly, kindhearted, and humble in spirit.
1 PETER 3:8 NASB

what really counts

Jesus Christ was kindness incarnate. He came to express it; lived to model it; died to offer it; and returns to impart it to us in the Holy Spirit.

LLOYD JOHN OGILVIE

How truly is a kind heart a fountain of gladness, making everything in its vicinity to freshen into smiles.

WASHINGTON IRVING

Character
Line Up and Wait

It is better to be patient than to be proud.

ECCLESIASTES 7:8 NCV

Here's a simple riddle almost anyone can answer: what is the one place that always has a line? The ladies' room. Whenever you really need to use a public restroom, it's usually filled with a busload of students or scenic-tour vacationers. So you end up doing what every other woman does—you stand patiently and wait your turn. Sometimes you have to line up and wait for the bathroom in your own home, too. Others may be in the shower. Someone else may be hogging the mirror. The sink might be full of Aunt Polly's unmentionables. The bathroom—public or private—can truly be a place to learn patience.

You know deep down that God is wonderfully patient. It's part of His nature. He doesn't have to work at being patient—He just is. As His child, God wants you to have that same quality of patience in your life, both as you wait for Him to work in your life and as you interact with others. The Bible often uses the word *long-suffering* interchangeably with the word *patience*. The underlying meaning here is that a person who is patient is also one who "suffers long" or hangs in there with someone else even when times are difficult or the individual becomes irritating and demanding. For example, a patient mom serenely waits while her little one does everything with dinner except eat it. A patient friend quietly listens to complaints or anecdotes that have been told time and again. A patient coworker explains the process to a slow learner one more time without hurry, frustration, or annoyance.

Though patience isn't a popular virtue in today's instant society, patience is necessary to the healthy growth of the church, too. God wants His people to exercise patience with everyone—pastors and leaders, family, friends, and other believers. The Galatians were reminded that patience is a fruit of God's Holy Spirit. Paul told the Corinthians that patience is a facet of love, and James assured his readers that patience is a clear reflection of faith and hope. The Bible also commended Abraham, Job, and the believers in Thessalonica and Asia Minor for their patience with one another.

When next you find yourself waiting for the bathroom, remember that learning to suffer long with others is a part of Christian discipleship. So "let patience have its perfect work, that you may be perfect and complete, lacking nothing" (James 1:4 NKJV).

Character
Line Up and Wait

What Matters Most...

◎ God and His will for you. God is patient; and He wants you to be just like Him in every way.

◎ Others and your patience with them. God urges you to hang in there in tough times with all people.

◎ Your Christian growth. Patience is a fruit of God's Holy Spirit that grows with time.

◎ What you do while waiting. You can fidget, fuss, and fume, or you can practice patience and watch love, faith, and hope grow.

◎ The example of others. Abraham, Job, Joseph, and Paul all learned patience.

What **Doesn't** Matter...

◎ How long you have to wait for anything.

◎ How busy you are. Everyone's busy. Being impatient only boosts your blood pressure, so give yourself a break.

◎ How many times you've been patient already today. Patience becomes easier if you give up the scorecard.

◎ How unpopular it is to practice patience. Discipleship involves becoming more like God.

◎ How hard it is to be patient with some people. God is patient with you. Ask for His help.

Focus Points...

Be joyful because you have hope. Be patient when trouble comes, and pray at all times.
ROMANS 12:12 NCV

Let us lay aside every weight, and the sin which so easily ensnares us, and let us run with endurance the race that is set before us.
HEBREWS 12:1 NKJV

As holy people whom God has chosen and loved, be sympathetic, kind, humble, gentle, and patient.
COLOSSIANS 3:12 GOD'S WORD

Always be humble, gentle, and patient, accepting each other in love.
EPHESIANS 4:2 NCV

what
really
counts

Patience governs the flesh, strengthens the spirit, sweetens the temper, stifles anger, extinguishes envy, subdues pride . . . Her throne is the humble and contrite heart, and her kingdom is the kingdom of peace.

BISHOP HORNE

On every level of life from housework to heights of prayer, in all judgment and all forts to get things done, hurry and impatience are sure marks of the amateur.

EVELYN UNDERHILL

Character
A Strong "Won't"

Do not join a crowd that intends to do evil.

EXODUS 23:2 NLT

what really counts

A television sitcom shows a family around a dining table shouting and carrying on a verbal battle of frustration. A magazine cover, showing two adults seated at an overladen dining table, bears the headline "The Hidden Cost of Cholesterol." A snapshot of a child's first day at school reveals a dining room table in the background that looks like a dumping ground, filled with trash to sort, mail to read, and piles of work to do.

Examples like these dining room disasters abound in today's busy society—some are worse, some are better, but many dining areas are out of control. Unfortunately, your life can mimic an out-of-control dining area too. People push and pull at you to do or be or go or come or give or take or whatever, until you're so frazzled and frustrated that you want to push everything away. You might have a good relationship with friends or family, but find yourself unable to say no to temptations whenever someone pushes an extra helping of guilt on you—eat this, do this, take this, you can always use this. And what woman hasn't felt like a dining-table dumping ground, overloaded with everyone else's concerns and chores in addition to your own.

Don't despair. He knows how to help you bring self-control to those areas of your life that seem out of control. After all, God helped Joseph run away from sexual temptation with Potiphar's wife. He helped David stand up to friends who urged him to kill King Saul when he had the chance. And God helped Paul look past hurtful words so that the apostle actually said good things about those people who had told lies about him.

The key to such self-control comes not from a strong will, but from a strong won't—I won't forget my commitment to God; I won't neglect to pray about the things that push me over the edge; I won't ignore God's presence in my life; I won't listen to the voice of anger, evil, frustration, or temptation. Self-control takes work, but it is an aspect of Christian discipleship that God through His Holy Spirit can grow in you. So start today. Ask God to send His Holy Spirit to help you "keep your eyes focused on what is right" (Proverbs 4:25 NCV). Then watch self-control begin to overtake the out-of-control in your life.

Character
A Strong "Won't"

What Matters Most...

- A steadfast commitment to God. No life can be fully in control unless it is first placed under God's control.

- A concerted effort in prayer.

- A clear sense of God's presence. He is always near, so you can access His power.

- A willingness to turn away from temptation.

- A dependence upon the Holy Spirit. When you allow yourself to be controlled by the Holy Spirit, you'll find peace.

What Doesn't Matter...

- The size of your dining area. Just let that area of your home remind you to seek God's help in self-control.

- What triggers your out-of-control feelings or actions. Being out of control is an indicator of your need for God's touch.

- That you're not a Bible hero. Joseph, Paul, and David started out weak in self-control issues, but learned to trust God with their lives. You can too.

- Your weak will. A strong will isn't the truest way to self-control. Your commitment to following God is.

Focus Points...

Keep your eyes focused on what is right, and look straight ahead to what is good. Be careful what you do, and always do what is right. Don't turn off the road of goodness; keep away from evil paths.
PROVERBS 4:25–27 NCV

The grace of God that brings salvation ... teaches us to say "No" to ungodliness and worldly passions, and to live self-controlled, upright and godly lives in this present age.
TITUS 2:11–12 NIV

Prepare your minds for service and have self-control. All your hope should be for the gift of grace that will be yours when Jesus Christ is shown to you.
1 PETER 1:13 NCV

what really counts

We should not be like other people who are sleeping, but we should be alert and have self-control.
1 THESSALONIANS 5:6 NCV

If you would learn self-mastery, begin by yielding yourself to the One Great Master.

JOHANN FRIEDRICH LOBSTEIN

We can have power over ourselves only when we have submitted to the Spirit's control and power in us. Christ's control is the basis of self-control.

LLOYD JOHN OGILVIE

225

Character
Laundry Lessons

> Those who are not holy will not see the Lord.
>
> HEBREWS 12:14 NLT

Once or twice a week (or maybe more frequently, if you live with children), a *chugga-chugga-whoosh-whoosh* sound emanates from your laundry room. Though some might sort through their dirty laundry to find the cleanest of the dirties to wear one more time, jeans and T-shirts, sheets and towels, socks and underwear need regular washing to make them look and smell fresh and clean, ready for use again.

The Bible uses the example of dirty and clean laundry to illustrate the cleansing needed in a believer's heart. Zechariah had a dream of the high priest Joshua standing before the Lord. The only problem was, Joshua was wearing dirty clothes. Just as you wouldn't expect to find your pastor standing behind the pulpit during a worship service with his dirty gardening duds on, so also Zechariah was astounded to see Joshua standing in God's presence wearing such filthy clothes. In Zechariah's dream, God ordered the removal of

Joshua's dirty garments. Then God spoke directly to Joshua, saying, "I've taken away all of your faults and failings and will clothe you with new, clean robes."

Zechariah's vision of the dirty and clean clothes is a clear illustration of God's view of holiness. Sin and selfishness, disobedience and willfulness make God's children "like an unclean thing, and all our righteousnesses are like filthy rags" (Isaiah 64:6 NKJV). In other words, all the good works, good intentions, and good living of a good person are merely like a teenager wearing the cleanest of the dirties. All the goodness anyone does can't erase the filthiness of a willful heart. The only way to achieve true holiness of heart is to receive it from God as a gift, just as Joshua received the gift of his new clean robes.

To grow in Christian discipleship and receive God's gift of holiness, first get rid of your selfishness and disobedience. God had to remove Joshua's dirty clothes—his faults and failings—before the priest could receive God's gift of holiness—the clean, rich robes. In the same way, prayerfully ask God to cleanse you and forgive you for those things you've said or done that run counter to His will and way. Then picture yourself in Joshua's shoes. Watch God remove the dirty clothes and replace them with clean ones. Experience the gift of God's holiness, and rejoice in the feeling of a cleansed heart. You'll find it's an even better feeling than fresh, clean socks.

Character
Laundry Lessons

What Matters Most...

◎ God's requirement of holiness from all His people.

◎ God's view of holiness. Goodness is not the same thing as holiness. In fact, God views human goodness as filthy rags.

◎ God's gift of holiness. You can't earn it in any way. Holiness of heart comes through God's cleansing and forgiveness.

◎ Living a life of holiness. It involves a daily turning-away from anything that takes you out of God's will and way.

What Doesn't Matter...

◎ How much dirty laundry is in your laundry room. Let your laundry duties remind you of the cleansing your heart needs to become holy.

◎ How dirty you are on the outside. God promises a completely clean heart when you seek His forgiveness and holiness.

◎ How many good things you've done. Good people mean well, but human goodness doesn't compare to God's standard of holiness.

◎ How many times you've failed. God knows you, and He has promised to forgive you—again and again, always, no matter what.

Focus Points...

Wash me thoroughly from my iniquity, and cleanse me from my sin.
PSALM 51:2 NKJV

You were washed clean. You were made holy, and you were made right with God in the name of the Lord Jesus Christ.
1 CORINTHIANS 6:11 NCV

Jesus answered, "If I don't wash your feet, you are not one of my people." Simon Peter answered, "Lord, then wash not only my feet, but wash my hands and my head, too!"
JOHN 13:8–9 NCV

How much more, then, will the blood of Christ, who through the eternal Spirit offered himself unblemished to God, cleanse our consciences from acts that lead to death, so that we may serve the living God!
HEBREWS 9:14 NIV

what really counts

No amount of description really tells us anything about holiness; but an encounter with it shames and amazes, convinces and delights us, all at once.

EVELYN UNDERHILL

What a wonder is it to be clean again—knowing there is no spot God cannot totally eradicate! It is a miracle almost too marvelous to understand ... *We are clean.* Not in ourselves, but because of Jesus.

NEVA COYLE

What Matters Most to Me About
Character

Discipleship—personal growth in following God's will and ways—takes time, work, effort, and lots of prayer. Consider these thoughts as you seek to grow in discipleship.

⊙ *Draw a rough floor plan of your home, noting the rooms discussed in these meditations. Choose two of those rooms/discipleship traits you want to see change in your life. Review the suggestions given and compose a prayer for God's help to make these traits a growing part of your faith.*

_____

_____

_____

_____

_____

_____

_____

⊙ *Consider the following statements, recording the importance or meaning of each one to you: (a) God is unwilling to withhold forgiveness if you ask for it; (b) Without God, the fruit of kindness would be nonexistent; (c) No life can be fully in control unless it is first placed under God's control; (d) Though people think being good is good enough, God doesn't.*

_____

_____

_____

_____

_____

_____

⊙ *Take a few moments to remember God's past faithfulness to you during difficult times. Now consider a friend who may be having a tough time. Is there a way you can remind them of God's goodness in the past? Record here what happens when you share these remembrances together.*

_____

_____

_____

_____

_____

_____

_____

_____

_____

⊙ *Record one or two experiences in which negative attitudes have prevented you from enjoying life or relationships. What positive attitudes could have changed these experiences? How could the outcomes have been different?*

_____

_____

_____

_____

_____

_____

_____

_____

_____

When the Holy Spirit controls our lives, he will produce this kind of fruit in us: love, joy, peace, patience, kindness, goodness, faithfulness, gentleness, and self-control.

GALATIANS 5:22–23 NLT

PRAYER

An Introduction

> The LORD is near to all who call upon Him, to all who call upon Him in truth.
>
> PSALM 145:18 NKJV

what really counts

Shopping at the mall. Talking on the telephone. Instant-messaging over the Internet. Visiting across the back fence with a cup of coffee. You name it—best friends spend time talking together, whenever and in whatever ways they can.

To become best friends with God, you need to spend some time talking with Him. According to the Bible, the best way to do that is through prayer. Prayer is your direct line to God, your means for connecting with Him at any time of the day or night with never a worry about a lack of signal or an Internet time-out glitch. Your prayers of praise, confession, and concern for self and others give you the opportunity to grow in your relationship with God, to bring those specific needs to the One who can do something about them. Because God promises to hear the prayers of His children and to respond to them, your prayers help strengthen your faith in your loving heavenly Father. And when you pray, God's answers can change situations, lives, and you, too.

Prayer is not just a nice-to-do, once-in-a-while thing, either. The habit of prayer is a need-to-do facet of your spiritual life. Prayer allows God's will to be done and brings glory and honor to His name. Prayer draws you nearer to God and helps you learn more about His will for your life. So get to know your heavenly best friend a bit better. Take some time and pray.

God will do nothing but in answer to prayer.
JOHN WESLEY

Prayer
Prayer Is Needful

Seek the LORD and His strength;
seek His face continually.

PSALM 105:4 NASB

Are you a meal skipper? A sleep cheater? A pill popper? Hopefully your answer to each question is a resounding "No!" for researchers have determined it is physically unhealthy for a person to skip meals (even when trying to lose a few pounds); to cheat yourself out of a good night's rest (even when behind in your work); or to take lots of pills to perk you up, ease your pain, or help you get to sleep (even when worn-out, achy, or overstressed). There is a healthier way to ease stress, calm down, and drop those extra pounds. You don't need a pill or a program—all you need is prayer. According to documented evidence, prayer and meditation can reduce stress levels and increase your ability to fall asleep faster. Prayer and meditation have also proved helpful for those wishing to revise unhealthy lifestyle habits. If you want to be physically healthy, prayer is needful.

Prayer is needful if you want to be spiritually healthy, too. Prayer—time spent with God seeking His guidance, presence, grace, and forgiveness—is an essential part of every believer's life. Without prayer, any relationship with God will falter because vital communication will be cut off. And when communication with God breaks down, disaster looms.

The Gibeonites had heard about Israel's conquest of Jericho. They believed their city would be destroyed next, so they worked out a scheme to fool the Israelites. Wearing ragged clothes and carrying rancid food, men from Gibeon lied to Joshua and said they were from a far country. They asked for an alliance with Israel, a peace treaty between their two nations. Unfortunately, "the men of Israel tasted the bread, but they did not ask the LORD what to do" (Joshua 9:14 NCV). Joshua went ahead and agreed to the Gibeonites' terms. Three days later, the Israelites found out they had been duped. Their misguided decision could have been averted if Joshua and his men had prayed. Instead, the treaty with the Gibeonites brought God's people trouble for many years.

To stay out of trouble and on track spiritually, make prayer a habit. God wants you to come to Him in prayer on a regular basis, whether in times of need or times of worship. He is your heavenly Father. For you to grow as His child, you need to talk to Him—every day, about everything.

Prayer
Prayer Is Needful

What Matters Most...

◎ Recognizing that a regular time of prayer can have a positive effect on both your physical and spiritual lives.

◎ Remembering that prayer gives you a chance to connect with God and gain His forgiveness, grace, and perspective.

◎ Understanding that without prayer, there is no communication with God. Major problems and misdirection in your life can result from such a lack of communication.

◎ Talking to God every day, about anything and everything that's on your heart. For you to grow as God's child, you need to talk to Him.

What Doesn't Matter...

◎ Whether or not you've made poor decisions without praying first. Learn from your experience and pray before any decision.

◎ Whether or not you are consistent in prayer. You'll find the more often you pray, the easier it becomes.

◎ Whether or not you've thought prayer was essential to your life. Without prayer, your relationship with God will falter.

◎ Whether or not you have anything important to pray for. Spend time in God's presence, and share your heart.

Focus Points...

Dear friends, build yourselves up in your most holy faith and pray in the Holy Spirit.
JUDE 20 NIV

Pray in the Spirit at all times with all kinds of prayers, asking for everything you need. To do this you must always be ready and never give up. Always pray for all God's people.
EPHESIANS 6:18 NCV

Be alert at all times. Pray so that you have the power to escape everything that is about to happen.
LUKE 21:36 GOD'S WORD

Jesus told them a story showing that it was necessary for them to pray consistently and never quit.
LUKE 18:1 MSG

what
really
counts

To bathe one's face every morning in the dew of heaven by prayer and communion, is the sure way to obtain true beauty of life and character.

CHARLES SPURGEON

Go boldly to God. He desires your prayers and has commanded you to pray. He promises to hear you, not because you are good, but because He is.

WILLIAM TYNDALE

Prayer
Prayer Is Answered

Call to Me, and I will answer you.
JEREMIAH **33:3** NKJV

Honk! Honk! The blaring blast from the dump truck resonated between the buildings on the busy city street. The four-year-old bystanders at the crosswalk didn't seem to mind. In fact, they were responsible for the noise. While waiting with their teacher at the crosswalk, the students had spied the dump truck coming around the corner. They began to wave and jump up and down. Some of them called out, "Beep! Beep!" while others vigorously pumped their fists in the air, pulling on the invisible cord of an air horn. The dump truck driver saw the students, waved a "hello," and roared past the cheering crowd with his earsplitting salute. Yippee!

What a picture of answered prayer. Think about it. When you stand on the street corners of your circumstances, you always have choices. You can wait for life's changes to come whenever they will, never really expecting anything from God. You can stand and contemplate the cracks in the sidewalk of life, hoping things will get better, but not expecting much. Or you can be like the children at the crosswalk, actively bringing your needs to the One who can do something about them.

Why? God longs to answer the prayers of His children. When Moses was unsure how to lead the Israelites, he asked God directly, "What should I do with these people?" And God answered him, giving him clear direction on how to guide the Israelites. Hannah had had trouble conceiving a child, so she took her need to God. A year later she could sing, "I prayed for this child, and the LORD has granted me what I asked of him" (1 Samuel 1:27 NIV). God may hold back His answers to prayer if disobedience, selfishness, injustice, or disbelief fills your heart. But when your prayers are offered in faith, obedience, humility, and with a right spirit, God stands ready to answer your call, for He promises to answer the prayers of His children.

Prayer is your avenue to God's heart. Since you are His child, He hungers to hear what's troubling you, what gives you great happiness. He yearns to give you guidance and direction so that you can grow in your faith and find success in your endeavors. His answer to your prayer can be like the sounding of a heavenly air horn, for God "is Lord of all and richly blesses all who call on him" (Romans 10:12 NIV).

Prayer
Prayer Is Answered

What Matters Most...

◉ Remembering that prayer is your avenue to God's heart. He wants to love you, help you, guide you, care for you.

◉ Understanding that God may hold back answers to prayer if unforgiveness or willfulness fills your heart.

◉ God won't force you to pray. You always have choices, but when you make prayer a priority, God stands ready to come to your aid.

◉ Knowing that prayers offered in faith and righteousness are prayers that move God to action.

What **Doesn't** Matter...

◉ What you pray about. If it's troubling you, pray. If you're excited about it, pray. Tell God everything.

◉ That you may feel selfish asking God for personal needs. God longs to provide for you as a loving Father. Take your needs to Him in prayer.

◉ That you've not received the answers you wanted in prayer. Remember, God won't say yes if it's not for your best. Trust Him to do what's right for you.

◉ How you react to answered prayer. Emotional responses aren't the issue. Seeing God actively involved in your life is the true blessing of answered prayer.

Focus Points...

The reason you don't have what you want is that you don't ask God for it.
JAMES 4:2 NLT

You will call upon Me and go and pray to Me, and I will listen to you.
JEREMIAH 29:12 NKJV

Before they call, I will answer; and while they are still speaking, I will hear.
ISAIAH 65:24 NKJV

I tell you, whatever you ask for in prayer, believe that you have received it, and it will be yours.
MARK 11:24 NIV

what really counts

The LORD is not too weak to save you, and he is not becoming deaf. He can hear you when you call. But there is a problem—your sins have cut you off from God.
ISAIAH 59:1–2 NLT

Unless there is some impediment on our part, we shall infallibly obtain what we ask, or something else more expedient for us, or it may be both together.

LORENZO SCUPOLI

Good prayers never come creeping home. I am sure I shall receive either what I ask or what I should ask.

JOSEPH HALL

241

Prayer
Prayer Is Precise

When you pray, you should pray like this.

MATTHEW 6:9 NCV

When Barb learned that her husband was going to run some errands, she asked him to pick up a new thimble for her. To make sure that her husband located the correct item, Barb described the thimble, its approximate price, where to find it in the store, and what the packaging might look like. She was very specific in her request and thereby pleased with the result when her husband returned home.

What Barb knew about husbands, errands, and thimbles applies to prayer, too. The more specific you can be when you pray, the better you will recognize and appreciate the package when God delivers His answer to you. Too often God hears vague or purposeless prayers from His children: *bless my family and friends; thanks for everything You do; forgive my sins.* While God listens and responds to these prayers when you pray them, it can be hard for you to clearly see when and how God answered your prayers if they were initially vague or imprecise.

what really counts

242

Consider this: a warring nation once invaded David's hometown and abducted his family. Rather than waste time on vague prayers, David prayed specifically about his need, asking God whether or not he should pursue the enemy and whether or not he would be successful in rescuing his family. Because David prayed so specifically, he was able to recognize God's direct answer and receive the guidance he needed to save his family. By praying specifically for your own needs, you can more clearly see God's outstretched hand of willingness to answer your prayers, too.

Try beginning your prayer time with adoration to God for what He has done for you, for the ways He is moving within your church, your home, your job. Be specific. Then turn your attention to ways you might have disappointed God. Confess your sins and seek His forgiveness. But don't be vague here, either. God already knows the truth. You can't fool Him, so be honest and specific. Confess your need for guidance about a particular situation, or ask for help for a special need. Then finish your prayer time with explicit thanksgiving, naming names of individuals for whom you're thankful, listing circumstances or situations in which God has proved His faithfulness to you. Such specific, substantive prayers will result in obvious, direct answers. And direct prayers and answers will ignite your faith, too.

Prayer
Prayer Is Precise

What Matters Most...

- Remembering that God hears your prayers whether they are specific or vague.

- Praying about the things that matter to you. God cares about you. Since you can't fool Him, why not pray about things that really matter?

- Finding time to praise God, for all He is, does, and provides.

- Understanding that by praying specifically for your own needs, you will more clearly see God's outstretched hand of willingness to answer your prayers.

What Doesn't Matter...

- Bossiness. Specific prayers are not telling God what to do. God always has the option to answer any specific prayer with a yes, no, or wait.

- Topics. Pray about anything. The main point of specific prayer is that you take whatever is on your heart and bring it to God.

- Unfamiliarity. It doesn't matter if you've never prayed specifically before.

- Time limits. Specific prayers don't need to be long.

Focus Points...

Ask, and it will be given to you; seek, and you will find; knock, and it will be opened to you. For everyone who asks receives, and he who seeks finds, and to him who knocks it will be opened.
MATTHEW 7:7–8 NKJV

Jesus asked him, "What do you want me to do for you?" He said, "Lord, I want to see." Jesus said to him, "Then see. You are healed because you believed."
LUKE 18:40–42 NCV

We have not stopped praying for you and asking God to fill you with the knowledge of his will through all spiritual wisdom and understanding.
COLOSSIANS 1:9 NIV

what really counts

Until now you have asked nothing in My name. Ask, and you will receive, that your joy may be full.
JOHN 16:24 NKJV

Thou art coming to a King, large petitions with you bring; for his grace and power are such. None can ever ask too much.

JOHN NEWTON

If you pray for bread and bring no basket to carry it, you prove the doubting spirit which may be the only hindrance to the gift you ask.

DWIGHT L. MOODY

245

What Matters Most to Me About
Prayer

Prayer is the best way to share your heart with God and for God to share His heart with you. He knows you, loves you, and wants to spend time with you. Grow closer to Him through prayer and as you journal your thoughts below.

◉ *God wants to have a relationship with you through the give-and-take of prayer. Reread the Scriptures in this section, and let God speak to your heart. Record here what you sense Him saying to you about prayer and your relationship with Him.*

_____

_____

_____

_____

_____

_____

_____

_____

◉ *Jesus made prayer a high priority when He was on this earth. Recognizing that prayer can have health benefits for your physical and spiritual lives, list some ways you can make prayer more of a priority in your life.*

_____

_____

_____

_____

_____

_____

_____

◉ *When you pray and harbor bad feelings in your heart, God will not hear you. However, if you pray with a heart full of forgiveness, you can be assured of God's answers. Knowing the truth of both those statements, what confession do you need to make to God right now? What do you want God to do for you? What answers to prayer do you need Him to confirm in your heart?*

_____

_____

_____

_____

_____

_____

_____

_____

◉ *Specific prayers bring specific answers. List three or four specific prayers here. By faith, let God work on them. Covenant with Him to revisit these prayers at a later date to record the answers He's given.*

_____

_____

_____

_____

_____

_____

_____

_____

Don't worry about anything; instead, pray about everything. Tell God what you need, and thank him for all he has done.

PHILIPPIANS 4:6 NLT

SIN

An Introduction

> Glory and strength to Christ, who loves us, who blood-washed our sins from our lives.
>
> REVELATION 1:5 MSG

what really counts

It comes in many forms. It can sneak up on you or fiercely attack. It may look good at first, but its slow poison only robs you of spiritual vitality. What is it? The Bible calls it sin.

Sin—that willful choosing of what you want irrespective of what God wants—results from giving in to a temptation to do this or that. Such temptations may involve a sharp pull to go in this direction, say a hurtful thing, look at something lewd, or engage in something unpleasing to God. Though temptation is not wrong in itself, allowing yourself to stand too near temptation for too long can weaken your resolve to do what God wants you to do.

Giving in to wrongdoing is not something people want publicly declared, either. If you do or say something you know is displeasing to God, your first reaction is often damage control. You try to minimize the bad and put a good spin on things. Or you tell a little white lie to cover up the bigger mistake. However, such secretive behavior doesn't fix whatever you're trying to hide.

Do what God wants. To live the way God wants you to live, you should make a conscious effort to run away from temptation while you still can. But if you should do something displeasing to God, be up front with Him about it. Ask for His forgiveness, for God's forgiveness is the only remedy to sin's slow poison.

> Sin is the only thing that God abhors. It brought Christ to the cross, it damns souls, it shuts heaven, it laid the foundations of hell.
> THOMAS BROOKS

Sin
Naughty Gnats

> When he lived on earth, he was tempted in every way that we are, but he did not sin.
>
> HEBREWS 4:15 NCV

Have you ever plowed through a cloud of gnats when you're all sweaty from a jog or a brisk walk? Gnats seem attracted to your perfume, body spray, or makeup. Those pesky little no-see-ums try to fly up your nose or get stuck in your hair. You shake, you swat, you sputter and spit, but it's almost impossible to get rid of those gnats unless you duck and run away.

Pesky gnats are a lot like the swirling harassment of temptation—the enticement to do something that is not pleasing to God. Everyone has to deal with temptations of different kinds: lewd thoughts, lies, the lust for things you cannot have, etc. The Bible reminds you temptation itself is not wrong—even Jesus faced temptation. However, Jesus didn't give in. He knew that giving in to temptation is wrong. Such willful wrongdoing violates the Bible and may lead others to do wrong too. When you give in to temptation and do something unpleasing to God, your faith wobbles; your close relationship with God is broken. To stay on track and live the way God wants you to live, you need to be alert to temptation and know what to do about it.

The Bible suggests you can avoid temptation's tug if you do the same thing you do with those naughty gnats—duck and run, or, in spiritual terms, pray and flee. When tempted to lie, cheat, steal, or do something displeasing to God, pray. Ask God to keep you from doing anything that would make Him unhappy. The Bible promises He'll "never let you be pushed past your limit; he'll always be there to help you come through it" (1 Corinthians 10:13 MSG).

Don't forget to run, too. Temptation will buzz around you until you either give in or run away. Don't give temptation a second look or think about it for an instant. Choose instead to follow God's guideline to flee temptation, running away from it as fast as you can, by closing the book, changing the channel, thinking about something else. Fill your mind with what is right, good, and honoring to God. Though running away from temptation might seem simplistic, it is a wise decision advocated by Paul, Peter, and Jesus, and practiced by Joseph when Potiphar's wife made lewd advances. Don't give in to the gnats of temptation and do what displeases God. Duck your head instead in prayer, and run away.

SIN

Sin
Naughty Gnats

What Matters Most...

◎ Knowing that everyone has to deal with temptation in some way or another, at some time or another.

◎ Understanding that temptation is not sin. Yielding or giving in to temptation crosses the line into sin's territory.

◎ Recognizing that willfully choosing your own way instead of doing things God's way violates the Bible and can also hurt others or cause their faith to waver.

◎ Remembering that running away from temptation is the best way to avoid falling into it. To stay out of sin, run away from temptation; run toward God.

What Doesn't Matter...

◎ What kinds of temptation you face. Different things tempt different people. Yet all need to learn to duck and run.

◎ How strong you think you are at standing up to temptation. Your strength will fail at some point. God's won't.

◎ How long you've been a Christian. Temptation can sneak up on anyone at any time in any number of guises.

◎ What day it is. Temptation doesn't take holidays. It can show up on good days or bad days, special days or ordinary days. Be prayerful. Be ready to duck and run.

Focus Points...

God himself does not tempt anyone. But people are tempted when their own evil desire leads them away and traps them. This desire leads to sin, and then the sin grows and brings death.
JAMES 1:13–15 NCV

Run away from the evil young people like to do. Try hard to live right and to have faith, love, and peace, together with those who trust in the Lord from pure hearts.
2 TIMOTHY 2:22 NCV

Control yourselves and be careful! The devil, your enemy, goes around like a roaring lion looking for someone to eat. Refuse to give in to him.
1 PETER 5:8–9 NCV

what really counts

When Christians find themselves exposed to temptation they should pray to God to uphold them, and when they are tempted, they should not be discouraged. It is not a sin to be tempted; the sin is to fall into temptation.

DWIGHT L. MOODY

The temptation once yielded to gains power. The crack in the embankment which lets a drop or two ooze through is soon a hole which lets out a flood

ALEXANDER MACLAREN

Sin
Not-So-Secret Secrets

Take note, you have sinned against the LORD; and be sure your sin will find you out.

NUMBERS 32:23 NKJV

what really counts

Sherry had a secret: she colored her strawberry-blonde hair. She always waited until she was alone to touch up her graying locks. However, one day an unexpected phone call added ten minutes to the color processing time. The hair dye box had warned: "brighter colors obtained with longer processing time." That label was right. Those extra minutes turned Sherry's curls redder than a clown wig. Now everyone knew Sherry's secret.

Achan had a secret too—a secret sin. When the ancient Israelites destroyed the city of Jericho, God ordered them not to keep any of the plunder from the city. Achan disobeyed, keeping some clothing, gold, and silver for himself. He buried the booty under his tent, believing no one would be the wiser. Days passed; nothing happened. But then, when the Israelites met their next enemy on the battlefield, they were soundly defeated. Many Israelites were killed. God informed Joshua that Achan had disobeyed His instructions concerning Jericho. So Joshua said, "Tell me what you have done; do not hide it from me" (Joshua 7:19 NIV), and Achan confessed. Only after Achan was punished for his secret sin was God's judgment lifted from an entire nation.

All people hide something. Your graying roots may hide under hair color. You may not smile broadly to hide some crooked teeth. You may hide emotional hurts or disappointments. Sadly, you may also hide a secret sin or two. You know the ones—the things polite people don't talk about openly; the degrading behaviors you keep repeating even though you wish you didn't; the bad choices that reinforce walls between you and God. Though these secret offenses may seem harmless at first, when allowed to continue over time, the bolder and bigger they become. One tiny fib can become a string of lies; petty larceny can escalate to grand theft; one flirtatious interplay can lead to an extramarital affair.

Keeping your secrets buried takes an emotional toll on you too, robbing you of the joy of living. Because the secret offenses you try to cover up often can have consequences as visible as Sherry's dyed hair or the Israelites' botched battle, why not give yourself a break? God already knows everything, so stop whatever you're doing that displeases Him. Pray for His forgiveness. Ask Him to help you break free from your secret sins. Give up the secrets and live your life with renewed peace, assurance, and joy.

SIN

Sin
Not-So-Secret Secrets

What Matters Most...

- Realizing the consequences of continued secretive wrongdoing.

- Remembering that bad choices build walls and break down your relationship with God.

- Understanding that there is no way to excuse or cover up willful wrongdoing.

- Knowing that keeping your secrets buried takes an emotional toll on you. Stop whatever you're doing that displeases God. Turn to Him for forgiveness—and live.

What Doesn't Matter...

- What faults and failings are troubling you right now. God knows everything. Don't try to hide. Ask Him for forgiveness.

- How big or small your secret offenses may be. Big or little, your failings are all the same to God. So quit 'em. Confess 'em. Don't waste another minute on them.

- That your secrets haven't hurt you so far.

- How well you think you can handle secret faults and failings. Such secrets leave telltale marks on your life, just as hair dye leaves color in curly locks. So come clean. Confess your hidden sins to God.

Focus Points...

You have set our sins in front of you. You have put our secret sins in the light of your presence.
PSALM 90:8 GOD'S WORD

Destruction is certain for those who try to hide their plans from the LORD, who try to keep him in the dark concerning what they do! "The LORD can't see us," you say to yourselves. "He doesn't know what is going on!" How stupid can you be?
ISAIAH 29:15–16 NLT

Wait until the Lord comes. He will bring to light things that are now hidden in darkness, and will make known the secret purposes of people's hearts.
1 CORINTHIANS 4:5 NCV

what really counts

How can I know all the sins lurking in my heart? Cleanse me from these hidden faults.
PSALM 19:12 NLT

One danger of secret sin is that a person cannot commit it without its being eventually betrayed into a public sin. If a person commits one sin, it is like the melting of the lower glacier on the Alps; the others must follow in time.
CHARLES SPURGEON

A little sin, unrepented of, will damn; as one leak in the ship, if it be not looked to, will sink it.
THOMAS WATSON

257

What Matters Most to Me About
Sin

Sin puts up a wall between you and God. Forgiveness tears that wall down brick by brick. Consider the weighty things of sin and temptation as you record your thoughts to these questions.

◎ *Fire officials suggest having an escape plan in case fire breaks out in your home. Using this suggestion as a starting point, list some temptations that you easily give in to. What escape plan could you devise and follow whenever these temptations arise?*

_____

_____

_____

_____

_____

_____

_____

◎ *Find 1 Corinthians 10:13 and James 1:13–15. Rewrite these verses here in your own words. Record your feelings about them, too. Whenever tempted, return to these words for assurance that God can help you overcome the pull of sin.*

_____

_____

_____

_____

_____

_____

◉ *Sin is not something to be trifled with, but rather admitted, repented of, and asked forgiveness for. Can you think of a time when you made excuses for your sin instead of repenting for it? What did this sidestepping do to your reconciliation with God?*

_____

_____

_____

_____

_____

_____

_____

_____

◉ *Secret sins sometimes involve hidden agendas like blaming others for putting temptation in your path. Have you ever wiggled out of admitting to a sin by shifting the blame to someone else? How did this affect your relationship with God and with those who received the blame?*

_____

_____

_____

_____

_____

_____

_____

_____

If you do not do what is right, sin is crouching at your door; it desires to have you, but you must master it.

GENESIS 4:7 NIV

RELATIONSHIPS

An Introduction

> Honor your father and your mother, that your days may be prolonged in the land which the LORD your God gives you.
>
> EXODUS 20:12 NASB

what really counts

The fifth commandment that God gave to Moses on the mountain deals with family, with the respect that children should give their parents. Unfortunately, in today's society, many families have forgotten to keep this fifth commandment, resulting in the disastrous disintegration of the family. Though God intended families to be a safe haven, to be a place of love and caring, all too often families today are places of pain and anger, stress and struggle.

Yet the Bible gives all families a promise of hope. God can bring blessing and a true sense of belonging to even the most dysfunctional family. He can make any family—yours included—happier, more loving, kinder, and more caring. God is a God of miracles.

And God is a God who knows your needs. That's why He offers you the opportunity to be a part of a new family—His family. Being a daughter in your earthly family can be difficult at times. You can fall short of your parents' expectations or rub up against rough spots with your siblings. But God offers to make you a part of His family, to make you His daughter. As God's daughter, you'll always be loved, always be cared for, and always have Someone to trust. You'll be a member of your earthly family—with all its good and bad points—until the day you die. But you can become a member of God's family, too. And being God's daughter can change your life forever.

A happy family is but an earlier heaven.
SIR JOHN BOWRING

Relationships
Domestic Dysfunction

> Be an example to the believers in word, in conduct, in love, in spirit, in faith, in purity.
>
> 1 TIMOTHY 4:12 NKJV

Laura Ingalls and John Boy Walton had it great. Strong, moral dad. Wise, beautiful mother. Close-knit siblings. Fervent family ties. Problems that were surmounted by love and laughter. Who wouldn't want a family like theirs from Walnut Grove or Walton's Mountain?

what really counts

Sadly, many families today experience situations vastly different from these television settings. Domestic dysfunction causes some families to approach problems with verbal or physical fights, name-calling, or harsh punishments. Other families disrespect their elders or look the other way when another family member is mistreated. Still other families outwardly seem to have everything together, yet live their lives as individual islands, neglecting one another and lacking love or personal interaction with each other. Psychologists define all these behaviors as types of abuse, stating that the psychological wounds caused by these behaviors are deep and lasting, often scarring hearts and minds for years.

Regrettably, families have always had trouble getting along. The Bible tells the stories of Amnon, who physically

262

abused his sister Tamar; of Athaliah, who killed her own children and grandchildren out of jealousy; and of Hagar, who nearly died fleeing from Sarah's cruel mistreatment. Because God values all life, any mistreatment, violence, neglect, or exploitation of another's life is wrong. And because God designed the family unit to be a place of love, trust, encouragement, and safety, He doesn't want dysfunction to be your family's way of life. He doesn't want the effects of such behaviors to exercise control over your daily existence. The problems in your family life can be overcome. God offers you and your family peace and wholeness, blessing and belonging.

How? The road to family harmony starts with prayer, with admitting your need for Him, for His powerful control over those things in your family relationships that you feel powerless to change. You *can* change some things, though, like your attitude. Ask God to help you be more loving, sensitive, respectful, and encouraging. Purpose in your heart to refrain from hurtful behaviors toward other family members. To resolve the pain of past situations, seek a counselor with whom you can be honest about your experiences and feelings. Work on forgiving those in your family who have mistreated you, and determine with God's help to seek ways to restore kindness and caring. Your family can become happier with prayer, time, and God's intervention. With His help, no domestic dysfunction is too great to overcome.

Relationships
Domestic Dysfunction

What Matters Most...

⊚ Understanding that many families don't live picture-perfect lives, even though God designed the family to be a place of love, trust, encouragement, and safety.

⊚ Realizing that mistreatment by a family member can be devastating and carry long-lasting consequences.

⊚ Remembering that God values all life.

⊚ Believing that God can intervene to restore and renew any family that seeks His help, His grace, His power, His forgiveness, and His love.

What **Doesn't** Matter...

⊚ Your social status. You're not alone. But God's love can put an end to your family struggles.

⊚ Your anger. If you've suffered family mistreatment, give up the anger, for anger won't make things right.

⊚ Your embarrassment. Mistreatment by another family member can be upsetting. Ask God to heal the hurt.

⊚ Your guilt. You may have mistreated another family member. God still loves you. Seek His forgiveness. Then seize any opportunity to make things right with the one you've wronged.

Focus Points...

Look on victims of abuse as if what happened to them had happened to you.
HEBREWS 13:3 MSG

Those who use and abuse each other, use and abuse sex, use and abuse the earth and everything in it, don't qualify as citizens in God's kingdom.
1 CORINTHIANS 6:9–10 MSG

Exploit or abuse your family, and end up with a fistful of air; common sense tells you it's a stupid way to live.
PROVERBS 11:29 MSG

Treat younger men like brothers, older women like mothers, and younger women like sisters. Always treat them in a pure way.
1 TIMOTHY 5:1–2 NCV

Every person we meet in the course of a day is a dignified, essential human soul, and we are guilty of gross inhumanity when we snub or abuse him.

JOSHUA LOTH LIEBMAN

Nothing is won by force. I choose to be gentle. If I raise my voice, may it be only in praise. If I clench my fist, may it be only in prayer. If I make a demand, may it be only of myself.

MAX LUCADO

Relationships
Daughters of God

[Jesus] said to her, "Daughter, your faith has made you well. Go in peace."

MARK 5:34 NKJV

what really counts

She had been troubled for years with a chronic hemorrhage, yet she was so unimportant in her community that those who chronicled her illness never recorded her name. One day this unnamed woman skirted the lakeshore, quietly edging her way toward the front of a crowd to catch a glimpse of Jesus. She never wanted to bother Him, to call attention to herself. But as the crowd jostled her, an opportunity came, so she reached out and touched the corner of Jesus' robe.

Matthew, Mark, and Luke record versions of this story, giving extra details about the day and the miracle that followed. But the best part of this story is not the woman's miraculous recovery. The best part is a single word. With one word, Jesus drove away the woman's dark clouds and gave her sunshine, gave her the blessing of peace. With one word, Jesus wrapped her in love and took her into His heart. That one word? *Daughter.*

Daughter. That word is life-changing. If you've ever had a tough day, a bad week, or a rotten month, you know how much a kind word can mean. But God has more than kind words in store for you. He offers you a reason to stand up and cheer, to smile and laugh, for all women who put their trust in God are His daughters. That means you, too. Not only are you a daughter of your earthly family, you can also be a daughter of God, a daughter with a heavenly Father—if you'll trust Him. You can be a daughter of grace, peace, and mercy if you'll open your heart to God. You can have a heavenly Father who is strong, generous, caring, and kind. You only have to touch God's heart with prayer and ask Him to make you His child.

When you pray such a prayer, wonderful things happen. Just as human daughters bear the genetic marks of their parents—eye color, hair color, etc.—so God's spiritual daughters bear the spiritual marks of their heavenly Father. When you become His daughter, you'll be forgiven, made holy and righteous. As God's daughter, you're cleansed, complete, and inseparable from His Spirit. As God's daughter, you're heir to His kingdom, you're called to His purpose. But best of all, as God's daughter, you're loved for eternity. That one word— *daughter*—can change your life forever.

Relationships
Daughters of God

What Matters Most...

◎ Realizing the blessings and benefits inherent in being God's daughter: forgiveness, peace, love, and purpose.

◎ Remembering that all women who put their trust in God are God's daughters too.

◎ Knowing that a simple prayer can change your life. Open your heart to God. Ask Him to make you His child. Then rejoice that you are God's daughter.

◎ Recognizing that as a daughter of God you will be loved and cared for forever.

What **Doesn't** Matter...

◎ How sick or healthy you may be. Just ask God to make you His child.

◎ Whether or not you're loved and accepted by your own human family. God offers you eternal acceptance into His family. Ask Him to make you His daughter.

◎ Whether or not you're well known or respected in the community.

◎ Which human family member you most resemble. Your physical family resemblances may fade one day, but your spirit is eternal. As God's daughter, your spirit will always resemble Him.

Focus Points...

God loved us and chose us in Christ to be holy and without fault in his eyes. His unchanging plan has always been to adopt us into his own family.
EPHESIANS 1:4–5 NLT

You can tell for sure that you are now fully adopted as his own children because God sent the Spirit of his Son into our lives crying out, "Papa! Father!" Doesn't that privilege of intimate conversation with God make it plain that you are not a slave, but a child?
GALATIANS 4:6–7 MSG

You are no longer strangers and foreigners, but fellow citizens with the saints and members of the household of God.
EPHESIANS 2:19 NKJV

In his goodness he chose to make us his own children by giving us his true word.
JAMES 1:18 NLT

You are a child of the King Himself, through Jesus. You are royal. You're a daughter of the King!

ELISA MORGAN

Which would you prefer? To be king of the mountain for a day? Or to be a child of God for eternity?

MAX LUCADO

What Matters Most to Me About
Relationships

There are positives and negatives about every family—every family, that is, except God's family. Reflect on your two families—both earthly and heavenly—as you consider the following thoughts.

◉ *Family members can fuss at one another and say things that hurt, things that can drive a wedge into the relationship. Have you said things to another family member that you regret? Is there someone to whom you need to apologize? Record your observations here. What steps can you take to restore family harmony?*

_____

_____

_____

_____

_____

_____

_____

◉ *Respecting family includes the way you speak to them when you're with them as well as what you say about them to others. When you're away from your family, do you gossip about their faults with other people? List some ways in which you have disrespected your family, noting ways you can change those behaviors and build your family up.*

_____

_____

_____

_____

_____

_____

All women are daughters, and all women are part of a family. Knowing that God wants all families to be places of love, trust, encouragement, and safety, what do you need to do to be a better daughter to your parents or a better sister to your siblings? How can you make your ideas a reality?

_____

_____

_____

_____

_____

_____

_____

_____

Record here some reasons to appreciate your status as a daughter in your earthly family. Now consider your status as a daughter of God. How does your heavenly family relationship as God's daughter compare to your earthly family relationship? What facets of being God's daughter can you apply to your daily relationships with family today?

_____

_____

_____

_____

_____

_____

_____

_____

As for me and my family, we will serve the LORD.

JOSHUA 24:15 NCV

SIGNIFICANCE

An Introduction

> How blessed is God! ... Long before he laid down earth's foundations, he had us in mind, had settled on us as the focus of his love, to be made whole and holy by his love.
>
> EPHESIANS 1:3–4 MSG

what really counts

With the first soft breezes of spring, garage sales mushroom in neighborhoods across the country. Tables and blankets are laden with sale items that used to fit, used to be useful, or used to have special meaning for their owners. Now the primary significance of these items revolves around how much they're worth to someone else.

Some women subconsciously believe they are just like garage sale items—significant, valuable, or important only because of their relationship to someone else. While women serve important roles as moms, coworkers, friends, or relatives, real worth in life—real importance and significance—involves much more than just what a person can do or be for someone else. Finding personal significance in life invariably means coming to grips with the real you—the person that God has created you to be. You're more than what you do or what folks see on the outside. You're a one-of-a-kind creation, a distinctive, unique woman, with a heart that longs to connect with her Creator.

You are important to God. He knows all about you—when you get up, when you go to bed, what you're thinking right now. You were created by Him and bear His image. You have been given the gift of eternal life. "Indeed, the very hairs of your head are all numbered" (Luke 12:7 NIV). Find your significance in God, and you will find significance in all life itself.

> Each person has a special importance as God's creation. When God moves into a person's life, that person's value becomes infinite, eternal, and unchanging because of the One who lives within.
> JOSH MCDOWELL

Significance
Distinctly Different

If you're content to simply be yourself, your life will count for plenty.
MATTHEW 23:12 MSG

what really counts

Have you ever mistakenly sprayed your hair with air freshener or underarm deodorant instead of hair spray? While you may have made that embarrassing mistake once or twice, you probably have never tried to gargle with your favorite fragrance. The size and shape of a perfume bottle tell your fumbling fingers in the half-light of early morning that this is not a bottle of mouthwash. In fact, the distinctive difference in the shape of each perfume container signifies to a woman's rushed touch which bottle will give her the scent of a woodland arbor or the fragrance of tropical flowers.

God is the originator of differences. He built distinctive differences into all areas of His creation. Fish are different from birds so that each can inhabit different locales. Even the stars in the sky harbor amazing differences. Though to the naked eye all the stars look alike, in the last few centuries scientists have developed telescopes advanced enough to see and study the differences between individual stars. Yet God knew about the differences between those stars when He created them. To God, difference is not something to abandon or alter. Distinctive differences are significant, essential parts of God's plan.

So, too, your distinctive differences set you apart from other people. Your personality quirks and traits, your fingerprints, eye color, or even the shape of your toes makes you, you. No other woman processes her thoughts exactly as you do; no one else has the same cowlick. You are one-of-a-kind, unique among God's creation. And you are significant to God and to His plan because of that uniqueness. He has a plan and purpose for you and your life that only you and your distinctiveness can accomplish. What you perceive as a personal limitation could be an asset to Him. So ask God to show you how He can use your differences for His honor and glory. Examine the talents and skills you possess. Consider your personality and the way you interact with others. Look for opportunities to use these distinctive differences to touch others' lives and share God's love.

Like a perfume bottle, you are distinctly different and unique. And because you are God's creation, you can gratefully accept your individuality, your distinctiveness. Praise God for your uniqueness in all its facets, because you are "fearfully and wonderfully made" (Psalm 139:14 NIV). Today, thank God for you.

Significance
Distinctly Different

What Matters Most...

- ◎ Recognizing that God can use distinctive differences for His honor and glory.

- ◎ Knowing that distinctive differences are significant, essential parts of God's plan.

- ◎ Realizing you—differences and all—are important to God.

- ◎ Understanding that God created you the way He wanted you to be.

- ◎ Finding God's plan for your life that only you and your distinctiveness can accomplish.

What **Doesn't** Matter...

- ◎ Your physical limitations. God can use your physical limitations for His glory.

- ◎ Your insecurities. God has given you abilities, gifts, and talents to use for Him.

- ◎ Your personality. God can work through any personality type to accomplish His will.

- ◎ Your failures or shortcomings. God often uses the flawed or unimportant to fulfill His plans and bring honor to His name.

- ◎ Other people's opinions. God's opinion is the one that counts; He made you the way He wants you.

Focus Points...

What a miracle of skin and bone, muscle and brain! You gave me life itself, and incredible love. You watched and guarded every breath I took.
JOB 10:11–12 MSG

You created my inmost being; you knit me together in my mother's womb. I praise you because I am fearfully and wonderfully made.
PSALM 139:13 NIV

We are God's masterpiece. He has created us anew in Christ Jesus, so that we can do the good things he planned for us long ago.
EPHESIANS 2:10 NLT

what really counts

With your very own hands you formed me; now breathe your wisdom over me so I can understand you.
PSALM 119:73 MSG

God made you in a marvelous way! . . . From your toes to your nose, you are the handiwork of God.

ELISA MORGAN

You're a masterpiece! Isn't that another reason for us to be lavish with our praise? You are God's child; you are beautiful; you are talented; you are a true gift to life!

SUE BUCHANAN

Significance
Fresh Paint

> Man looks at the outward appearance, but the LORD looks at the heart.
>
> 1 SAMUEL 16:7 NIV

Chances are, you spend some time each day combing your hair, applying some makeup, or tweezing a stray chin hair. Yet advertising suggests you need to do more to be younger, sexier, or more successful. Gray hair, brittle nails, and sagging skin never reflect the true you, the ads seem to say.

While it is true that a little fresh paint can make an old barn look better, wearing a certain brand or fixing a certain blemish will not make any significant changes to the real you. According to the Bible, your worth and meaning in life aren't found in temporary externals like "fancy hair, gold jewelry, or fine clothes" (1 Peter 3:3 NCV). Scripture insists that true personal significance comes from the inside, from your heart's commitment to God.

In the Old Testament, when Samuel journeyed to Bethlehem to anoint Israel's new king, Jesse brought out seven sons for the prophet's perusal. These young men were tall, dark, and handsome. Samuel was impressed, but God wasn't. Drop-dead gorgeous wasn't the clincher in God's book to choosing a new king. Outward appearances are temporary. They can be altered—by age, paint, plastic surgery, or other means. A person's heart, however, is eternal. The heart reveals the true character and worth of that individual. When Jesse's sunburned youngest was brought in from the field, immediately God said, "He is the one" (1 Samuel 16:12 NIV). God had looked deep into David's inner being, found a man after His own heart, and appointed him leader of the people. David's life found new significance and meaning because his heart was fully committed to God.

You, too, can find renewed significance and meaning in life by changing your inner focus. Set your heart each morning just as you set your hair. Decide to seek God's direction daily, asking God's Spirit to flow through you in everything you do. Completely surrender yourself to your Creator's claim on your life. Put a little paint on the old barn if you like. Brighten up the clapboards with a touch of mascara or blush. Darken your roof's roots with haircoloring's finest, if that makes you feel better. But remember, what's inside the barn is more valuable than the barn itself. It's not what you look like on the outside that counts. To find true significance in life, work on making your heart—the inner you—beautiful.

Significance
Fresh Paint

What Matters Most...

◎ What's going on in your heart.

◎ Your personal relationship with God.

◎ Your commitment to following God in everything you do. True personal commitment comes from the heart.

◎ Changing your life focus to match God's will and way.

◎ Letting God work in your life to touch others, too. Ask God each morning to work through you.

What Doesn't Matter...

◎ How beautiful you are or aren't. Physical beauty isn't the measure of true beauty.

◎ Your age, weight, race, or shoe size. They are all just numbers.

◎ What others say you should look like, act like, be, or do.

◎ External add-ons like clothing, accessories, or hairstyle. Your significance comes from the inside.

◎ How others view you or perceive you to be. God knows who you really are on the inside.

Focus Points...

Know that the LORD Himself is God; it is He who has made us, and not we ourselves.
PSALM 100:3 NASB

He has made everything beautiful in its time.
ECCLESIASTES 3:11 NKJV

I want women to get in there with ... humility before God, not primping before a mirror or chasing the latest fashions but doing something beautiful for God and becoming beautiful doing it.
1 TIMOTHY 2:9–10 MSG

Charm is deceptive, and beauty is fleeting; but a woman who fears the LORD is to be praised.
PROVERBS 31:30 NIV

what really counts

You must display a new nature because you are a new person, created in God's likeness—righteous, holy, and true.
EPHESIANS 4:24 NLT

Whatever I am, Lord, You made me ... Lovingly, carefully, reverently, and exactly right.

JOY MORGAN DAVIS

Our created purpose is to let God's light shine through every facet of our being, expressing His colors and beauty through us in ways no one else can.

CONNIE NEAL

What Matters Most to Me About
Significance

Personal significance isn't found in externals. Your worth, importance, and meaning in life come from a realization that you matter to God. Let your heart connect with your Creator as you reflect on these thoughts.

◉ *How does the knowledge that the God of all creation cares about your life affect your feelings of significance, importance, or self-worth?*

_____

_____

_____

_____

_____

_____

_____

_____

◉ *Spend some time thinking about what makes you unique, one-of-a-kind. List two or three of these distinctions, journaling ways God could use them for His honor and glory.*

_____

_____

_____

_____

_____

_____

_____

what
really
counts

◉ *What three things can you do to develop the inner beauty mentioned in 1 Peter 3:4? How will these things change your significance to God and others? How will they change your attitude about yourself?*

_____

_____

_____

_____

_____

_____

_____

_____

_____

◉ *Compose a prayer to God, praising Him for the wonderful way in which He has made you.*

_____

_____

_____

_____

_____

_____

_____

_____

Your beauty should come from within you—
the beauty of a gentle and quiet spirit that will
never be destroyed and is very precious to God.
1 PETER 3:4 NCV

WORK AND CAREER
An Introduction

> Hard work always pays off; mere talk puts no bread on the table.
>
> PROVERBS 14:23 MSG

what really counts

The bird kept at it all day. Twigs, leaves, and dry grasses soon intertwined around a porch light, forming a nest for the soon-to-arrive bird family. When the eggs were laid, the mother bird had a brief chance to rest. In a matter of days, though, she was busier than ever, feeding cheeping chicks at all hours of the day and night. A mother bird's work is never done.

And neither is yours, or so it seems. Though you have many choices in life, one constant never changes: you'll always have some work to do, whether you work inside or outside the home. Though women today have more career options than their ancestors, the decisions affecting what kind of job you will hold can sometimes seem overwhelming, for women work for different physical, emotional, and financial reasons. Yet God wants you to remember that there are also spiritual reasons for work. God wants all women in all walks of life to honor Him in everything they do—including their work.

Just as the mother bird's natural abilities help her build a nest and care for her chicks, so your God-given abilities help you do certain tasks better than others. Since work isn't just for the birds, discovering your abilities and talents, your likes and dislikes, and your past work successes and failures could help you replace a job that is boring and unfulfilling with a career that will give you a feeling of success and satisfaction. So—get to work.

> Today, let us rise and go to our work. Tomorrow, we shall rise and go to our reward.
>
> RICHARD FULLER

Work and Career

Work's Reasons

Those who work hard will prosper
and be satisfied.

PROVERBS 13:4 NLT

what really counts

Women do things for many reasons. You may take the stairs instead of the elevator because you're trying to lose a few pounds. You may opt out of attending a midnight hockey game because you want your beauty sleep. You may choose to go on a short-term mission trip because you want to reach out to others with God's love.

You may choose to work outside the home, too, for you have employment choices—choices that most women in Bible times never had. Ancient Israelite women worked long hours grinding grain, harvesting fields, and selling items in the marketplace. Ancient homemakers carried water, kneaded bread, and sewed all the clothing their family needed. Though it was uncommon, some women worked outside the home. Ruth went through the fields after the harvesters, gathering bits of grain that might have been dropped or left behind. But these women never had the opportunity to run a business or work in nontraditional roles. Career options for women didn't exist in Bible times.

Things have changed with time. Women now have more career options. And, like their biblical counterparts, women still work hard, often balancing home and career responsibilities. Some work to keep food on the table, while others work outside the home to pay for life's extras. Some work to better themselves or stay current in their fields. And still other women work for the benefits that come with the job—insurance coverage, college tuition breaks, or ongoing training. Many women have chosen to stay at home and work as moms or homemakers, too. Yes, women work for many reasons.

Yet there are spiritual reasons to work too. Whether you have a job in or outside the home, all work is meant to honor God. Your work gives you an opportunity to get to know others and to share God's love with them. Work opens your eyes to loving as God loves, to seeing other people as He sees them. Whatever kind of work you do, know that *how* you do it matters, too. God wants you to work cheerfully, with all your heart, as if He were the one asking you to do the job, not some boss or family member. When you work at your tasks with these reasons in mind, you'll gain more than success, satisfaction, or stability from your employment. One day you'll also hear God say, "Well done, good and faithful servant" (Matthew 25:23 NKJV).

Work and Career
Work's Reasons

What Matters Most...

◎ Recognizing that there are many choices for women in the workforce today, and many reasons for making those choices.

◎ Being a worker who honors God in all things and thereby makes other people hungry to know Him too.

◎ Opening your eyes to those you work with, seeing them as God sees them, loving them as He loves them.

◎ Working at everything you do with a cheerful heart, as if God were the one asking you to accomplish the task.

What Doesn't Matter...

◎ Your knowledge of biblical customs and work.

◎ Your family background. If your work routine is different from your mother's, don't fret. God knows that.

◎ Whether you work in or outside the home.

◎ Who your coworkers are. You are to be God's light to each one—whether you're changing a diaper, teaching a class, driving a forklift, or doing anything else. All work should honor God.

◎ How much you make, what position you hold, or how much prestige your job confers on you.

Focus Points...

You should be a light for other people. Live so that they will see the good things you do and will praise your Father in heaven.
MATTHEW 5:16 NCV

Go to work in the morning and stick to it until evening without watching the clock. You never know from moment to moment how your work will turn out in the end.
ECCLESIASTES 11:6 MSG

Be strong and do not let your hands be weak, for your work shall be rewarded!
2 CHRONICLES 15:7 NKJV

People should eat and drink and enjoy the fruits of their labor, for these are gifts from God.
ECCLESIASTES 3:13 NLT

what really counts

You spend more of your waking hours engaged in work than in any other activity. Can you imagine that your gracious heavenly Father . . . would want you to dread the largest slice of your life? Not a chance.

ROBERT WOLGEMUTH

Our forefathers succeeded because their goal was not material wealth alone but glory to God. Their mundane work was as sacred as the frontier parson's. They believed whatever they did was God ordained.

TOM HAGGAI

289

Work and Career
The Recipe of Work

Settle down and get to work.
Earn your own living.

2 THESSALONIANS 3:12 NLT

Every recipe made by every chef contains some of same elements. For example, every recipe needs an ingredi that will bind things together. It may be flour or cornstar an egg or cheese, or maybe a vegetable purée. Every rec needs moisture—water, fruit juice, cream, etc. And ev recipe needs seasonings, too—salt, pepper, or others. Yet extra things that a chef folds into a creation—chocolate k or leavening, shiitake mushrooms or pasta—will ultimat determine whether the finished product will be a cookie cake, or a casserole.

In the same way, the work women do, the jobs they ho all share certain elements. All work, regardless of whether task is performed in the home, in an office, or on a high w requires time, effort, and skill. Yet the extras you bring to yo work—your education, talents, and personal ethics—v determine how well you will do your job. Just as you c adjust a recipe to fit your personal tastes—add more salt;

290

less sugar—so you often can adjust your work to make it more satisfying for you.

Here's how: God has given you special talents and abilities. If you're unsuccessful in your work or have a job that's uninteresting, it's possible you're working outside your abilities. In Paul's day, Lydia was renowned for her textile creations. During Nehemiah's time, Shallum's daughters exhibited construction skills, helping to rebuild part of Jerusalem's wall. You'll probably find the most success and satisfaction in a job that complements your God-given abilities. Not sure what those are? Ask God to help you uncover your talents. Take time to consider your past successes. Look at the jobs you've held that you've enjoyed. What are you good at? You might see a pattern that suggests a job that's a good fit for your abilities.

Yet there's more to you and your work than just your talents. To make work more satisfying, you might need to make some job adjustments. Are you where God wants you to be, doing what He wants you to do? Has your education prepared you for a specific field? Does your job honor God or compromise your ethics? Do you need to better balance home and career by working fewer hours? If you fold these extra observations into the recipe of your work, you'll surely get more than a cake or a casserole. You might just end up with a more fulfilling career.

Work and Career
The Recipe of Work

What Matters Most...

◉ Recognizing that all work requires time, effort, and skill whether you work in or outside the home.

◉ Remembering that God has given you special talents and abilities to use to benefit yourself and others.

◉ Realizing that finding fulfillment in your work may mean making some job adjustments.

◉ Being willing to seek God's direction when it comes to your work and career.

What Doesn't Matter...

◉ How well you cook. You may not have the ability to be a chef, but the talents God has given you can be used to honor Him in your work.

◉ Where you work. Ask God to show you where He wants you to be and what He wants you to do.

◉ How long you've worked at your job.

◉ How many talents you have. One talent or many, God wants you to use those abilities.

◉ What career you choose. If the job you choose honors God, uses your talents, and brings satisfaction, go for it.

Focus Points...

Observe people who are good at their work—skilled workers are always in demand and admired; they don't take a back seat to anyone.
PROVERBS 22:29 MSG

Work hard and cheerfully at whatever you do, as though you were working for the Lord rather than for people.
COLOSSIANS 3:23 NLT

Live a quiet life, minding your own business and working with your hands, just as we commanded you before. As a result, people who are not Christians will respect the way you live, and you will not need to depend on others to meet your financial needs.
1 THESSALONIANS 4:11–12 NLT

Whatever presents itself for you to do, do it with all your might, because there is no work, planning, knowledge, or skill in the grave.
ECCLESIASTES 9:10 GOD'S WORD

Your natural abilities are God's suggestions for your life's work.

CLYDE NARRAMORE

In order that people may be happy in their work, these three things are needed: they must be fit for it, they must not do too much of it, and they must have a sense of success in it.

JOHN RUSKIN

What Matters Most to Me About
Work and Career

As you record your observations, remember that all work—
whether done in the home or outside it—is to be done cheerfully as unto God. He has given you your job. Honor Him with
your effort.

◎ *Where do you spend most of your working hours—in the home or outside it?
List several reasons why you spend your working hours doing what you do. Are
you pleased with the result of these observations? What do you need to change
to feel better about how you spend your work time?*

_____

_____

_____

_____

_____

_____

_____

_____

◎ *Think about your work. How has your job given you an opportunity to get to
know others? How has your work opened your eyes to the needs of others, to
loving them as God loves them? What do you need to change in your attitude
toward your job to be more cheerful or honoring to God in your work?*

_____

_____

_____

_____

_____

_____

_____

Think about all the jobs you've had. What jobs were most fulfilling? Why did you enjoy these jobs so much? If money were no object, what job would you absolutely love to have? What patterns can you see in these employment situations? How can this information impact your current position?

_____

_____

_____

_____

_____

_____

_____

_____

_____

List some of your strengths and weaknesses, your God-given talents and abilities. How well does your work fit your talents? Do you feel successful in your job? Are you doing what God wants you to do? What adjustments can you make to your work to make it more satisfying and honoring to God?

_____

_____

_____

_____

_____

_____

_____

_____

_____

My heart took delight in all my work,
and this was the reward for all my labor.
ECCLESIASTES 2:10 NIV

MONEY AND FINANCES

An Introduction

> You shall remember the LORD your God, for it is He who gives you power to get wealth.
>
> DEUTERONOMY 8:18 NKJV

what really counts

Buy up railroads and utilities. Corner the market on related properties. Put up houses and hotels. Own the richest tracts on the game board to guarantee financial security. If only the management of money and finances were as simple as this favorite family board game. Although you control the outgo of your income, God is the One who holds the monopoly on your money.

When you search the pages of the Bible, you find He is the One who gives you the power to earn wealth. God is the One who blesses you and makes you successful. He is the One who provides for your needs. He is your source for everything. The dream and craving to acquire more money or more financial security will leave you empty and unfulfilled. God wants to show you a better life focus for your money that will bring the satisfaction and contentment you seek.

Too often debt gets in the way of contentment and financial security. Though shopping expeditions can be fun, the bills that come due after spending sprees can become a burdensome debt. The Bible adds that being in debt is like being a slave to someone. Because God doesn't want you to be a slave to anyone or anything except love, controlling debt is one of the first steps to financial freedom. You can monopolize board games for family fun, but for ongoing financial wellness, deep-down contentment, and overflowing godliness, let God control your money.

> All our money has a moral stamp. It is coined over again in an inward mint. The uses we put it to, the spirit in which we spend it, give it a character which is plainly perceptible to the eye of God.
>
> THOMAS STARR KING

Money and Finances
Elusive Dreams

> Trust in your money and down you go! But the godly flourish like leaves in spring.
> PROVERBS 11:28 NLT

what really counts

Ever have one of those days when you wish you had new dishes, the latest fashions, two weeks—no, make it three—on a tropical island with attentive staff to bring you whatever you want whenever you want it? Ah, that would be the life. But then reality hits. You'd have to be as rich as King Midas to make those dreams come true. If only you had all the money you could ever want, then life would be wonderful.

Really? King Solomon was wealthier than any person in his day. His yearly income in gold alone was almost $11 million. Silver—in any amount—was as unimportant to Solomon as a penny on the sidewalk. He didn't even bother to count it. Yet, despite his riches, Solomon said it was "absurd to think that wealth brings true happiness" (Ecclesiastes 5:10 NLT). Those who love money, riches, or possessions will be discontent, because they will always want more.

The apostle Paul took Solomon's realization one step further. Having money wasn't wrong, Paul said; using it selfishly was. Constantly grasping for more money or possessions would only make someone as cranky as a begging toddler in a supermarket checkout line. You've seen those children, pestering Mom with "I want! I want!" Even if Mom gives in and buys the treat, the child won't be satisfied. Next week's grocery trip will inevitably play a rerun of the "I wants." Paul realized he needed a different focus when it came to money. Rather than succumbing to the "I wants," Paul turned his attention to what God wants when it comes to money. Paul knew everything he had came from God's hand, so his money should be used for whatever God wanted. Money should be used to do good for others, to help the poor, to spread the gospel. Paul said whatever amount of money God provided for him was exactly what he needed. With that life focus toward money, Paul could passionately say he was content in any circumstance.

It's the same for you. When money or possessions become the focus of your life, contentment will fly out the window. But when your wants and desires for your income are in line with God's wants and desires, and when your trust is placed in His ability to provide for your needs, then you are truly rich in godliness. And that's something money can't buy.

Money and Finances
Elusive Dreams

What Matters Most...

- ◎ Realizing that money can buy some nice things, but contentment isn't one of them.

- ◎ Remembering that those who focus their lives on money will never have enough. For true satisfaction, focus your eyes on God and His provision for your needs.

- ◎ Understanding that everything you have comes from God's hand.

- ◎ Turning your attention to what God wants you to do with your money. Use it to do what God wants.

What Doesn't Matter...

- ◎ How much money you make. Dollar amounts don't really matter; what you do with those dollars, however, does.

- ◎ What kind of car you drive. Cars, houses, and other possessions won't last forever. Your relationship with God will.

- ◎ Where you live. Big house or small. Apartment or rented room. For true contentment, where you live doesn't matter.

- ◎ How large your retirement account is. Money can disappear or be used up. Trust God for His provision.

Focus Points...

You can't worship two gods at once. Loving one god, you'll end up hating the other. Adoration of one feeds contempt for the other. You can't worship God and Money both.
MATTHEW 6:24 MSG

Take care! Protect yourself against the least bit of greed. Life is not defined by what you have, even when you have a lot.
LUKE 12:15 MSG

Lust for money brings trouble and nothing but trouble. Going down that path, some lose their footing in the faith completely and live to regret it bitterly ever after.
1 TIMOTHY 6:9–10 MSG

what really counts

Money can buy: A bed but not sleep. Books but not brains. Food but not an appetite. Finery but not beauty. A house but not a home. Medicine but not health. Pleasure but not peace. Luxuries but not culture. Amusements but not joy. A crucifix but not a Savior.

PAUL LEE TAN

True riches, of course, are totally unrelated to money or material reward ... The richest people I know are those who have given themselves unselfishly to other people.

TIM LAHAYE

Money and Finances
Debt Not Thyself

> If you are untrustworthy about worldly wealth, who will trust you with the true riches of heaven?
>
> LUKE 16:11 NLT

If financial counselors today could add a commandment to the ten God gave to Moses, it might be worded, "Debt not thyself, lest thou go broke." Though shopping and purchasing clothes, shoes, or household furnishings may be fun, facing the mailbox a month after a credit card spending spree can be a real eye-opener. Those plastic rectangles have ushered many to the brink of bankruptcy.

While some debt may be necessary or prudent, excessive debt can be financially disastrous. A home mortgage or college loan is a large debt to repay, but these debts are considered investments in your future. However, owing creditors more than you can pay off in two years for things you will wear out, use up, or give away is financially unwise. Your debt makes you a slave to a lender, and the widow of Shunem faced family disaster because of such debt. When she couldn't pay her creditors, they threatened to sell her children as slaves.

God doesn't want any of His children—including you—to be in bondage to anyone or to any lender.

Credit card debt raises extra concerns, too. Some buy on credit to cover unplanned purchases. Such impulse spending can indicate a lack of self-control, signifying that God's Holy Spirit is not working freely in an individual. Credit card debt can also indicate a lack of trust in God. If you charge a purchase on a credit card because you're not sure how God could provide the cash to pay for it, beware. You may be putting more trust in your ability to handle your debt than in God's ability to provide for your needs.

So what can you do about debt? Begin to reduce it by asking God to help you stop digging the hole of debt any deeper. Then start to save. An ant gathers a tiny bit at a time, but ultimately ends up with a full anthill. If you save a little from every paycheck, you'll soon have a tidy sum to cover unexpected expenses. Don't forget to pay off your creditors, too. Add extra amounts to the minimum payment on your smallest debt until it is completely paid. Keep this strategy up until all your debts are discharged. Finally, follow God's mandate to give back some of your income to Him. You'll find your life—and your pocketbook—will overflow with blessings in return.

Money and Finances
Debt Not Thyself

What Matters Most...

◉ Remembering that debt makes you a slave to a lender, and God doesn't want you to be in bondage to anyone.

◉ Realizing that impulse spending can indicate a lack of self-control, signifying that God's Holy Spirit is not working freely in your life.

◉ Understanding that excessive debt may indicate you're putting more trust in your ability to handle debt than in God's ability to provide for your needs.

◉ Following God's suggestions for financial wellness: pay off your creditors, save a little every month, and give back some of your income to Him.

What Doesn't Matter...

◉ Your age. Young or old, it doesn't matter. Debt can sneak up on anyone who is not careful.

◉ Your job. If you were to be unemployed tomorrow, a debt-load could sink your household. For family financial stability, don't increase debt. Pay off what you owe.

◉ Your perceptions. What you *want* may not be what you *need*.

◉ Your sex. Men and women are both guilty of overspending habits. But habits can be broken. Debt not thyself.

Focus Points...

Owe no one anything except to love one another, for he who loves another has fulfilled the law.
ROMANS 13:8 NKJV

Be careful about giving a guarantee for somebody else's loan, about promising to pay what someone else owes. You might get trapped by what you say; you might be caught by your own words.
PROVERBS 6:1–2 NCV

The rich rules over the poor, and the borrower is servant to the lender.
PROVERBS 22:7 NKJV

Pay everyone, then, what you owe. If you owe any kind of tax, pay it. Show respect and honor to them all.
ROMANS 13:7 NCV

what really counts

America has more things than any other nation in the world, and more books on how to find happiness.

W. E. SANGSTER

It should be our endeavor to keep as much as may be out of debt. Some sell their liberty to gratify their luxury.

MATTHEW HENRY

What Matters Most to Me About
Money and Finances

Sometimes it's hard to know when you've made making a living or retiring your debt more important than your relationship with God. Make a prayerful, personal inventory of your financial picture below.

◉ *How content are you with what you have, with what God has provided? How much time and energy do you spend on building your net worth? On building your relationship with God? Do you trust God to provide everything you need or do you rely on your financial securities and insurance policies?*

_____

_____

_____

_____

_____

_____

◉ *You are a slave to whatever controls you. How has your view of money made you its slave? Do you have trouble distinguishing between wants and true needs? How have you allowed your income, investments, or material possessions to become a burden? What are some things you can do to bring freedom to these areas of your life?*

_____

_____

_____

_____

_____

_____

what
really
counts

◎ *If you made a necklace from macaroni or cereal loops, adding one "bead" to the necklace for each $100 you owe a creditor, how heavy or long would your necklace be? What does this visual aid tell you about your indebtedness? What can you do right now to stop increasing your debt load? What steps must you take to eliminate debt from your life?*

_____

_____

_____

_____

_____

_____

_____

_____

◎ *Compose a prayer asking God to help you bring your finances into line with His guidelines. Be honest in your assessment of your ability to handle your income and debt. Then remember, God wants you to have one ongoing debt—loving others. Ask Him to show you ways to reduce your financial debt and to begin to build your debt of love.*

_____

_____

_____

_____

_____

_____

_____

_____

If they listen and obey God, then they will be blessed with prosperity throughout their lives. All their years will be pleasant.

JOB 36:11 NLT

HEALTH

An Introduction

> I will heal them; and I will reveal to them an abundance of peace and truth.
>
> JEREMIAH 33:6 NASB

what really counts

Information on health and lifestyle choices is more available today than ever before. Bookstores have expanded their sections on health and fitness. Health-related magazines have recorded increased subscriptions. In addition, medical Web sites are some of the most-sought-out locations on the Internet.

Researchers have published the results of the effects of different lifestyles on health, too. These reports conclude that a lifestyle lived in constant worry and fear can raise your stress levels, bring about the onset of major illness, and even shorten your life span. However, as a child of God, you possess a powerful antidote to living a life of worry and fear—the word of truth. Because fear is nothing more than a false expectation that appears to be real, telling yourself the truth as found in the Bible can be a way to unmask fears and remove their deleterious effects on your health.

But you don't always need the newest published book to find the best health guidelines. The Bible is full of guidelines for healthy living for all women. Because God created you, He knows what's best for you. You can consult the Bible to find out what to do to take care of your womanly body. Remember, though, that your health is not limited to physical issues. God is also concerned with your spiritual health. He has given you all the instructions you need to be healthy on all fronts—both physical and spiritual—within the pages of the Bible.

Half the spiritual difficulties that men and women suffer arise from a morbid state of health.
HENRY WARD BEECHER

Health
Not Sapped but Wrapped

Can all your worries add a single moment to your life? Of course not.
MATTHEW 6:27 NLT

what really counts

It starts small—a laugh line on your smiling face. But as you stare into the mirror each morning, that tiny wrinkle grows into a major worry. Is it deeper than it was yesterday? Is it growing longer? If it's left untreated for another week will you look like the poster girl for radical cosmetic surgery?

The scenario may be a bit exaggerated, but women often latch onto small concerns and turn them over in their minds until the small things become major worries. If those worries are allowed to fester and grow, they can become full-blown fears. While some fears may be good—a fear of slipping and falling may keep you safely off the icy winter streets—living a life filled with worry and fear is an unhealthy practice that can cause devastating consequences.

Sarah found this out when her husband, Abraham, fell apart with fear. Abraham and Sarah had traveled to Egypt seeking food during a terrible time of famine. However, upon arrival in Egypt, Abraham noticed that the king's officers were eyeing Sarah, for she was beautiful. Abraham got nervous. What if the officials wanted Sarah for the king's harem? The more Abraham thought about it, the more worried he became. Would they try to kill him so that they could take her? Truly afraid now, Abraham told Sarah to lie to the king's officials and say Sarah was Abraham's sister. That way, Abraham figured, both their lives would be spared. Sarah did as Abraham asked and was immediately whisked away into the king's palace. God intervened, but because of Abraham's unchecked worries and unresolved fear, he made a foolish decision that nearly cost him his wife and family.

The unhealthy lifestyle of persistent worry and fear can affect the quality of your life and shorten your life span, too. So if you're concerned about something, don't let your health get sapped. Instead, wrap that worry in the truth from the Bible so it can't grow into fear. For example, if your finances are stretched thin—tell yourself the truth, that God can "supply all your need according to His riches in glory" (Philippians 4:19 NKJV). If you're afraid of a new situation— tell yourself the truth, that God will show you what He wants you to do if you'll only ask Him. And, about those wrinkles— don't worry about those, either. They don't make you look monstrous. They make you look like you.

Health
Not Sapped but Wrapped

What Matters Most...

◉ Recognizing that unhealthy patterns of little concerns can become worries that grow into encompassing fears.

◉ Understanding that some fears can protect you from danger, but a lifestyle of worry can ruin your life.

◉ Remembering that unresolved worry and fear can blow things out of proportion, including your objectivity and good judgment.

◉ Accepting that worry and fear can have deleterious effects on your health, add to your stress, and shorten your life span.

What **Doesn't** Matter...

◉ How easy it seems to worry. Looking for truth and trusting God might not come naturally, but can become a habit with practice.

◉ How stressed you are or aren't. The truth of God's promises will send worry, fear, and stress scurrying.

◉ Whether you're young or old. Worry can strike anyone at any age. Let the truth of the Bible remove your worries.

◉ How healthy you are right now. Ill or healthy, keep your spirit healthy. Fight fear with God's truth.

Focus Points...

Cast your cares on the LORD and he will sustain you; he will never let the righteous fall.
PSALM 55:22 NIV

Do not worry about your life, what you will eat; nor about the body, what you will put on. Life is more than food, and the body is more than clothing.
LUKE 12:22–23 NKJV

Give all your worries and cares to God, for he cares about what happens to you.
1 PETER 5:7 NLT

Do not worry about tomorrow, for tomorrow will worry about itself. Each day has enough trouble of its own.
MATTHEW 6:34 NIV

what really counts

Have you ever taken your fears to God, got the horizons of Eternity about them, looked at them in the light of His love and grace?

ROBERT J. MCCRACKEN

Facing fears with a prayer on my lips and faith in my heart allows me not only to trust God more but also to experience victory that comes from no one but Him. Actually, that is a rather exhilarating way to stay fit.

MARILYN MEBERG

Health
Physically Female

I pray that you may prosper in all things
and be in health, just as your soul prospers.
3 JOHN 2 NKJV

George Bernard Shaw once quipped, "Think what cowards men would be if they had to bear children. Women are altogether a superior species." Whether or not you agree with Shaw's "superior species" assessment, all women, regardless of marital status or age, have to deal with the health and physicality of being female—premenstrual syndrome, a monthly cycle, menopause, etc.

what really counts

Being female in ancient Israel was a challenge. God was concerned about the well-being of all His children, so He issued some guidelines to restrict unhealthy practices and promote beneficial ones. Several of God's guidelines dealt specifically with the female issues of the menstrual cycle and childbirth because of their blood loss. Modern medicine now knows disease spreads easily via contact with germ-laden blood products. However, centuries before this medical discovery, God limited personal contact with a woman if "the discharge from her body is blood" (Leviticus 15:19 NKJV). A hemorrhage might indicate a more serious illness than a woman's menstrual cycle, so God's suggestion to quarantine all bleeding women helped prevent the spread of contagious disease.

After childbirth, God's guidelines kept a mother and child in seclusion for one to two months. During that time the mother was not allowed to work. No chores. No gardening. No cooking. While it might appear that God was being severe, medical science now sees the value of God's guidelines. Because childbirth is a strenuous process, rest is essential to recuperation. Less contact with well-meaning, germ-laden friends and relatives gives newborns and moms a healthier environment, too. And, a mother who doesn't have to rush right back to work will have more time to bond with her child and build stronger emotional ties to aid her child's future development. Therefore, God's guidelines for female health were not unrealistic. Rather, they were helpful, healthy, and caring.

Some of God's ancient guidelines—cleanliness, hygiene, diet, exercise—are still healthful practices to follow today. Yet the lessons behind God's suggestions for living a physically healthy life are important too. As you wash up, eat up, rest up, and follow the health guidelines found in the Bible, remember that He wants you to be spiritually healthy, too. Your heart needs cleansing from faults and failings; your spirit needs to feed on the Bible. You'll find rest in His presence and strength from daily prayer. As one of God's children, be physically female, but don't forget to be spiritually connected to Him too.

Health
Physically Female

What Matters Most...

◎ Remembering that God created you and understands the physical issues of being female.

◎ Following healthy practices and principles of cleanliness, hygiene, diet, and exercise.

◎ Keeping the healthy living guidelines God has given you to follow in the Bible.

◎ Understanding that God wants you to be physically *and* spiritually healthy. Do what it takes to be completely healthy—inside and out.

What Doesn't Matter...

◎ Your age. The Bible contains suggestions for healthy living for women of all ages.

◎ Your background. God's suggestions for healthy living apply to all persons regardless of ethnic or economic background.

◎ Your marital status. Married or single, you're a woman with a woman's needs. Check out the Bible for suggestions for staying healthy.

◎ Your career choice. Whether a stay-at-home mom or a career woman, your body needs all the care you and God can give it.

Focus Points...

God bought you with a high price. So you must honor God with your body.
1 Corinthians 6:20 NLT

Give yourselves completely to God since you have been given new life. And use your whole body as a tool to do what is right for the glory of God.
Romans 6:13 NLT

Don't depend on your own wisdom. Respect the Lord and refuse to do wrong. Then your body will be healthy, and your bones will be strong.
Proverbs 3:7–8 NCV

Training your body helps you in some ways, but serving God helps you in every way by bringing you blessings in this life and in the future life, too.
1 Timothy 4:8 NCV

The woman was made of a rib out of the side of Adam; not out of his feet to be trampled upon by him, but out of his side to be equal with him, under his arm to be protected, and near his heart to be loved.

Matthew Henry

God can use you even when you've living between estrogen and death. Age on, girls, the best is yet to be!

Barbara Johnson

What Matters Most to Me About
Health

By relinquishing a life bound by worry and fear and following God's guidelines for healthy living, you can be the healthy woman God created you to be. Consider the following thoughts as you seek to improve your health.

◉ *Record an instance where you allowed a concern to grow into a worry or fear. What feelings came to the surface in your thoughts and actions? How could the truth have affected that situation? What promise of God could you record here so you won't worry about that same concern again?*

_____

_____

_____

_____

_____

_____

_____

◉ *List some of your life's priorities. Are any of these concerns running you ragged? Causing you to worry? Affecting your health? What priorities need to change to give you less stress, less worry, and more time to spend on improving your spiritual health through Bible study and prayer?*

_____

_____

_____

_____

_____

_____

what
really
counts

◎ *Name some of the challenges you've faced in life because you are female. How have you addressed those situations? What else do you need to do to be more physically healthy? Whom could you ask to help hold you accountable as you seek to improve your physical and spiritual health?*

_____

_____

_____

_____

_____

_____

_____

_____

◎ *For good physical health, doctors recommend getting good food, exercise, and rest. For spiritual health, you need the food of the Bible, the exercise of Bible study, and the rest of prayer. Set some goals to follow for the next few months to incorporate these recommendations into your physical and spiritual health programs.*

_____

_____

_____

_____

_____

_____

_____

If you diligently heed the voice of the LORD your God and do what is right in His sight, give ear to His commandments and keep all His statutes, I will put none of the diseases on you which I have brought on the Egyptians. For I am the LORD who heals you.

EXODUS 15:26 NKJV